The Vanishing Tiger

The Vanishing Tiger

Wild Tigers, Co-predators & Prey Species

Vivek R. Sinha

SALAMANDER

To my wife Arati my constant companion in all my forays into remote forests, without whose encouragement my interest in wildlife photography would never have developed into a passion

A SALAMANDER BOOK

Published by Salamander Books Ltd.
The Chrysalis Building
Bramley Road
London W10 6SP
United Kingdom

A member of **Chrysalis** Books plc

ISBN 1 84065 441 4

Credits
Editor: Marie Clayton
Assistant Editor: Katherine Edelston
Designer: John Heritage
Production: Ian Hughes
Reproduction: Anorax Imaging Ltd
Printed and bound in Singapore

Additional captions
Page 1: This seven-month-old male cub had very unusual markings on his front legs.
Page 2-3: Sita hunting.
Page 4-5: Cub playing with mother.
Page 6-7: A tiger pair resting in Ranthambhore.
Page 8-9: A very large, angry tiger adopts a defensive posture before attack.
Page 10: This is Choti Mada (Younger female), daughter of Badi Mada (elder female), a well known tigress of Chuhri (wet land) of Kanha, who raised many litters in the Park. Choti Mada was resting in the meadow when our elephant happened to approach too close. She snarled viciously and we withdrew.

CONTENTS

> “Tiger, tiger, burning bright in the forests of the night, what immortal hand or eye dare frame thy fearful symmetry?”
>
> William Blake 1757-1827

FOREWORD

Till the middle of the 20th Century, in India tigers had been looked at over the barrel of a gun. They have been hunted with the camera since then. Among the most proficient among the camera ‘hunters’ is Vivek Sinha, whose photographic record of the tiger is indeed remarkable. Mr Sinha has wandered over the length and breadth of tiger land and in the process has acquired an impressive photographic insight into all aspects of the life of the tiger. The tiger, its habitat and its co-inhabitants all come alive in this singularly attractive book.

It is rarely that a photographer has any other interest than in obtaining the best possible image of his object of study. Vivek Sinha looks at not only the tiger, his main focus of

Above: *A nearly six-year-old tigress, cooling in water. In April 1998 we came across this tigress sitting in water at about 4 pm just inside a valley to the left of the road from Kisli to Kanha camp.*

attention, but also the many facets of the tiger's life in the wild. Each chapter covers a facet of the tiger and its environment. All those species which could be involved in the tiger's quest for food are covered in the photographic essay on co-predators. These lesser predators, though they may not present a major competition to the tiger's food supply, can still be a petty nuisance to the tiger in its search for food. Similarly all the prey from the regular to the occasional are covered in the photographic survey.

The tigers' varied habitat, the protected areas, are the haunts where Sinha has spent most of his time chronicling the life of an animal whose survival is in great jeopardy.

The book is indeed a splendid tribute to the tiger.

J C Daniel
Honorary Secretary
Bombay Natural History Society

“In the last 100 years or so, from a population of about 100,000, hardly 6,000 tigers remain in the world.”

INTRODUCTION

FROM TIME IMMEMORIAL, the tiger has been an object of great awe, reverence and superstition. It has an overpowering presence and its strength and ferocity are proverbial. It is deeply interwoven in the folklore and mythology of a number of countries where it is also a symbol of bravery. In India, it is closely associated with a feared Hindu Goddess, Durga, the slayer of demons.

Today its survival is in great jeopardy. In the last 100 years or so, from a population of about 100,000, hardly 6000 tigers remain in the world. Out of its eight subspecies, three have already become extinct in the last sixty years. In India, where 60 per cent of the total population lives, its number has declined by over 90 per cent within the last century. The

Right: *On 25 April 1991, we watched for nearly 45 minutes as a tigress stalked a herd of chital grazing on a plateau about six metres (20 feet) high at Bari Chuhri. The tigress here is crouching low, eyes focused on the grassy plateau where the deer were feeding. The stalk was a failure even though the tigress had successfully stalked the herd within 10 metres (30 feet).*

tiger, king of the forest, had once lorded over its territory for over a million years with no conflict with man, because there was adequate forest cover. There were large core areas and larger buffer zones, and the people surrounding the forest could easily obtain their sustenance from the buffer zones. Man respected the rights of the tiger and the tiger kept away from man.

Left: *On 29 March 2001, we had gone to Mukki, about 30 km (18.8 miles) from Kanha, and at Sondar Camp got the news that a tiger had been seen in Kanha. We returned via the Sondar tank and saw a very large tigress sitting on the road. We waited for about 20 minutes for her to move away. The tigress was looking around for some prey but then got up and entered the forest. We immediately heard sambar alarm calls and the tigress walked parallel to the road for some time, then crossed the road and went towards Umar Jhola area. We heard the intermittent alarm calls of sambar and chital, for sometime afterwards. Generally alarm calls are given when the carnivore is on the move and cease if it sits down.*

With the invention of firearms, the tiger was hunted in the name of sport. It could probably have survived this; its doom, however, was spelt by human encroachment in its territory in the name of land reclamation for farming, human resettlement, mining, large dams for irrigation and electricity, industrialisation, logging, etc. The forest and its denizens could not cry out and became easy spoil for those who, in their greed, saw easy money to be made out of the forest areas.

The tiger is said to have evolved about two million years ago in North China before it migrated to other countries. But the increasing demand for its bones and organs, sought for traditional medicines in its original homeland, has added a perilous question mark to its survival prospects. It is estimated that in India alone, one tiger is falling prey every day to poachers, who generate as much as $100,000 per kill for their clandestine masters.

With constant threat to its ever-diminishing and already fragmented habitat and with corridors gone, the depleted tiger population may soon come down to a level lower than required for the genetic diversity essential for survival of the species. It is feared that this level may be reached within the next couple of decades. Unless the conscience of the world is stirred by the sad plight of the tiger and the concerned countries show genuine commitment to preventing its extinction, the tiger may soon fade into just a memory. The wild tiger in its habitat then could, perhaps, be only seen and admired through photographic images.

Over the last two decades my wife, Arati, and I have tried to capture the beauty and life-style of this magnificent animal in the wild through the lens. Some of the images of the Bengal tiger are reproduced in this book, with the hope that they will give as much pleasure to the readers as the pursuit has given us.

“Being extremely fast and powerful, its very name has been derived from the classical Greek root for ‘arrow’.”

THE VANISHING TIGER

THE TIGER IS KNOWN to have evolved about two million years ago in the cold northern forests of the region now encompassing Siberia and northern China. Over time, probably due to the worsening weather conditions and lack of prey base, it was forced to spread out to warmer areas in the south and west. Some reached Korea and Manchuria and others moved through the central Asian wetlands to the west and southwest. The hostile mountain range of the Himalayas, stood as a serious barrier to their migrating into India. Tigers moving westwards through Central Asia, north of the Tibetan plateau, and south of Gobi desert found shelter in the region around Caspian Sea and eastern Turkey. Another stream moved southward from China and, circumventing the

Left: *The internationally famous tigress, called Sita, of the Chakradhara, Gopalpur, Fort and Jamunia areas of Bandhavgarh National Park, is seen sitting in her habitat of tall elephant grass in Chakradhara. She was born in 1982 near a very large sandstone sculpture of Lord Vishnu reclining under the hood of the mythological serpent, Seshnag. She remained the dominant tigress of the tourism zone, attracting visitors from all over the world. Over the years she gave birth to 18 cubs in 6 litters, the first litter of 2 males and a female being born in early 1986. Only 7 tigers survived to adulthood, the rest either died or disappeared. She was last seen on June 30, 1998, the day the park closed for four months for the rainy season (June to October) of 1998. She was then about 16 years of age, rather too old for the wild.*

Himalayas, moved into Indochina, Thailand and the Malaysian peninsula. Being good and strong swimmers, they crossed into the Indonesian islands of Sumatra, Java and Bali, but could not proceed to Borneo and Sulawesi as the intervening straits were very wide. Some of the tigers pushed westwards into Burma and finally about 10,000 years ago entered into India. The earliest evidence comes from sculpted tiger on seals of Indus valley civilization of Harappa and Mohenjodaro, placed at 2500 to 1700 BC

Folk Lore and Myths

The beauty, magnetic presence and tremendous power of the tiger, coupled with what appears its uncanny ability to appear and disappear at will in the forest, has made it an object of

Below: *Sita relaxing with four feet up exposing her white belly. Her father, called Daddy, sustained deep injuries when he was about 12 years old, while killing a porcupine. He was tranquilised by the Park authorities and 17 quills were removed but died three days later. Sita's mother remained in the habitat for about five years then left the area. Sita, one of two sisters, took over her range, while the sister, moved to the nearby territory of Bhadrashila.*

Right: *Sita yawns before moving away. After the death of her father, Daddy, in 1984 another tiger, named Banka, moved over as the territorial tiger and mated with her towards the end of 1985. The first litter of two male and one female cubs was born in early 1986. Only one male, named Narbaccha (male cub) survived, the other died. The female was named Hardia moved over to Bhadrashila, from where Sita's sister had moved out.*

Above: *Sita had killed a sambar near Charanganga, the perennial stream flowing through Chakradhara, in the early night of 12 April 1997. At that time she had three cubs, one male and two females, about eight months old. They had already fed and climbed up the Machai hill to rest and now she was feeding.*

great awe, reverence and superstition. The tiger has been interwoven in the folklore and mythology of many countries. Being extremely fast and powerful, its very name has been derived from classical Greek root for 'arrow'.

In China there are many stories such as, "The Tale of The Trusty Tiger", where a tiger was said to have saved a man who had fallen into a ditch so the man repaid by feeding it every year with a pig. Just like 'were-wolves', there are also myths about boys turning into tigers. The marking on the tiger's forehead is interpreted as the Chinese character 'Wang' meaning 'King' and commanded due honours. The tiger is

Above: *Close-up of the feeding tigress.*

one of the 12 animals in the Chinese Zodiac which is based on a 12-year cycle; the year 2010 will be the next year of the tiger. Korea is called "Land of the Blue Dragon and White tiger", and it is believed that a dragon guards the West and a tiger guards the east of the country. The tiger was also chosen as the symbol of 1988 Olympic games in Seoul. In Indonesia, there are tales of mythical times when a deal was made between the people and tigers to respect each other's territory - the forest for the tiger and the village and the agricultural lands for the people. In India, the tiger has permeated into many aspects of religion and culture; there are refer-

Left: *Sita quenching her thirst after a good feed.*

Below: *Sita lying near the kill keeping watch against the scavengers of the forest, which are always waiting for their turn.*

ences to tigers in the epic Ramayana and Mahabharata of the Vedic period of about 5000 years ago. The feared goddess Durga, slayer of demons, is always shown riding a tiger.

Habitat

The basic need of a tiger is protective cover, adequate prey base and water. Once these are available, it is unbelievably adaptable to a wide range of habitats - from scorching heat to freezing cold; from mangrove swamps to drier forest types; from mountainous cover to low lying forests and from lush evergreen forests to arid areas.

For more than a million years, the Siberian tiger has sur-

Right: *Sita's male cub reflecting at a waterhole.*

Below: *Sita's female cub leaping over a jungle stream. The tiger can dispatch small animals with a final spring and tremendous blow of the paw or lethal bite to the nape of the neck.*

"Not long ago, forest cover was large and the forests were interconnected with corridors permitting dispersal of the tiger population, thus ensuring genetic diversity."

Below: *Sita drinks at a waterhole in Chakradhara grassland. After feasting on a kill a tiger will go for a drink at the nearest waterhole and return to rest not far from the kill to keep watch.*

vived the snow and temperatures as low as -35 degrees C (- 31 degrees F) in the mountain regions of Amur basin and the coniferous, scrub oak and birch woodlands of eastern Russia. The Caspian tiger was once ranged throughout the reed-beds of the Caspian Sea up to the humid forests and grasslands of western Afghanistan, Iran, Mongolia, Turkey and the central regions of Russia. The Indochinese tiger lives in remote forests in hilly to mountainous terrain. The Sumatran tiger ranges from lowland forests to sub-mountain and mountain forests. It is also found in the thick forests of Burma and the dark and humid rain forests of Indonesia.

The Bengal tiger is found in a wide range of habitats from high-altitude, cold, coniferous forests in the Himalayas, to the world's largest mangrove swamps of the Sundarbans Tiger Reserve and from wet, evergreen forests of Assam to the thorny forests of Western Ghats. It also lives in heavy grass jungles, bamboo thickets and the dry scrubland of Central India and Rajasthan. It has been known to climb up to about 3960 metres (13,000 feet) in the central Himalayas to hunt domestic yaks.

Not long ago, forest cover was large and the forests were interconnected with corridors permitting dispersal of the tiger population, thus ensuring genetic diversity. There has been a sea change since then. The forestlands have now been heavily encroached upon and the corridors have disappeared, leaving behind only islands of tiger reserves.

Solitary Hunter

The tiger leads a very solitary and secretive life unlike the

Left: *Banka, the dominant tiger of the tourist zone and sire of the first two litters of Sita, sitting almost camouflaged among dried Sal leaves.*

Above: *Narbaccha, the male from the first litter of Sita sired by Banka, had moved over to Bathan area, but now and then he visited his mother's territory to make kills. Here he is sitting on the dodua hill, one of the hills surrounding Chakradhara grassland.*

Right: *Last stages of Narbachha yawning.*

Far Right: *Narbachha, reflected in a waterbody known as Ramtalaia, up in the Bandhavgarh hills.*

lion, which is a social animal. It has a highly developed vision about six times more powerful than man's, and an exceptionally acute hearing. These two attributes are essential to locate its herbivore prey, which also has almost matching senses. The prey species, however, have a sharper faculty of scenting than the tiger. This makes the tiger's task of finding its prey more difficult, especially in the dense undergrowth of the jungle where the tiger lives. In addition, the jungle has a very fine inbuilt alarm system, in which watch for a predator

Narbachha relaxing on dried sal leaves.

Right: *Sita showing affection to a cub, called Dau, in Chakradhara near Charanganga stream. Three cubs were born to Sita in October 1988, all males. This was her second litter sired by Banka. She was hiding them in a cave very high on the Bandhavgarh hills. A serious forest fire started in the Bathan area on 29 April 1989, which spread to the Bandhavgarh hills. One park elephant, Taramati, was badly burnt and died. The cubs were in the cave when the fire started. They were not seen until the 14 May 1989 when they looked very weak and starved. One of the cubs died and the other two survived to adulthood; they were named Balram and Dau, based on Indian mythology.*

is kept from the ground as well as the treetops. As soon as danger is sensed or a suspicious movement observed, the forest denizens are alerted to be on guard. The deer emit warning staccato calls of "Ku", "Ku", "Ku", the jungle fowls and pea fowls abruptly fly away cackling loudly and the monkeys and langurs jump from branch to branch cursing the predator. In addition, the prey species are too fleet-footed for the tiger to catch once they escape the initial charge of around 28 to 36 metres (92 to 118 feet).

The only chance for the tiger to catch its prey is to stalk it silently within 9 to 21 metres (30 to 70 feet) through dense cover with great stealth, crouching to a low profile, taking advantage of the natural camouflage provided by dark stripes on its yellow coat, and ability to freeze for long periods if the

Right: *Sita keeping a watch over her two sleeping cubs, Balram and Dau.*

Right: *The brothers, Balram and Dau were very close to each other. Balram suddenly disappeared on 27 November 1991 and Dau on 22 January 1992. It was feared that they were poached.*

“The tiger is a very efficient killer. It is packed with awesome strength and is endowed with an unmatched armament of claws and fangs and dagger-like canines”

Left: *Sita scolding one of her 15 month old cubs from her third litter of two male and two female cubs born in 1991. One cub was killed by a transient tiger and one just disappeared. Of the two who survived one was slightly lame and was known as 'Langda' (the lame one), the other was christened 'Taqdir' (the fate).*

Left: *We were searching for Sita and her 15-month-old cubs in the Chakradhara grassland. We were with Kuttappan mahout and his elephant called Toofan. At about 8 am a coughing roar of a tiger followed by a very high pitched squealing of a wild boar was heard from the foothill of Machai hill bordering Chakradhara. We hastened towards the disturbance to find Sita holding the throat of a wildboar and pinning it down. The boar was struggling wildly uttering the high-pitched painful cry. After 15 minutes or so the cry slowly ebbed and the struggle ceased but Sita kept her hold on the throat for another 15 minutes. Her hungry cubs were eagerly waiting along side and the tired tigress rested nearby as the cubs fed on the kill.*

prey gets suspicious. It is said that the tiger generally approaches its prey from downwind to avoid detection. Its rate of success is about one in twenty stalks; the rest end up in near misses or abandoning of the attempt on being discovered prematurely. Hence, out of sheer necessity, the species has to lead a solitary life (except when courting or with young), as the hunt would be almost impossible if attempted in groups.

Hunting Behaviour

The tiger hunts a wide range of prey: from various species of

Above: *Sita with a four to five-months-old female cub sleeping on her back in a small patch in Chakradhara on 10 April 1997. We heard some human-like sneezes, and after some searching we saw two more siblings hiding deep in the grass behind Sita . Probably their noses were being tickled by the grass.*

deer such as spotted deer, sambar, barking deer and swamp deer to wild boar and even bigger animals like gaur, *Bos gaurus*, young elephant, wild buffalo and rhinoceros. When driven by hunger, it is known to eat almost anything from frog, fish, bird or even other predators like leopard and bear. Its preferred food, however, is deer and wild boar. It varies its hunting tactics depending on the circumstances and the size of the prey.

The tiger is a very efficient killer. It is packed with awesome strength and is endowed with an unmatched armament of claws and fangs and dagger-like canines. It can dispatch

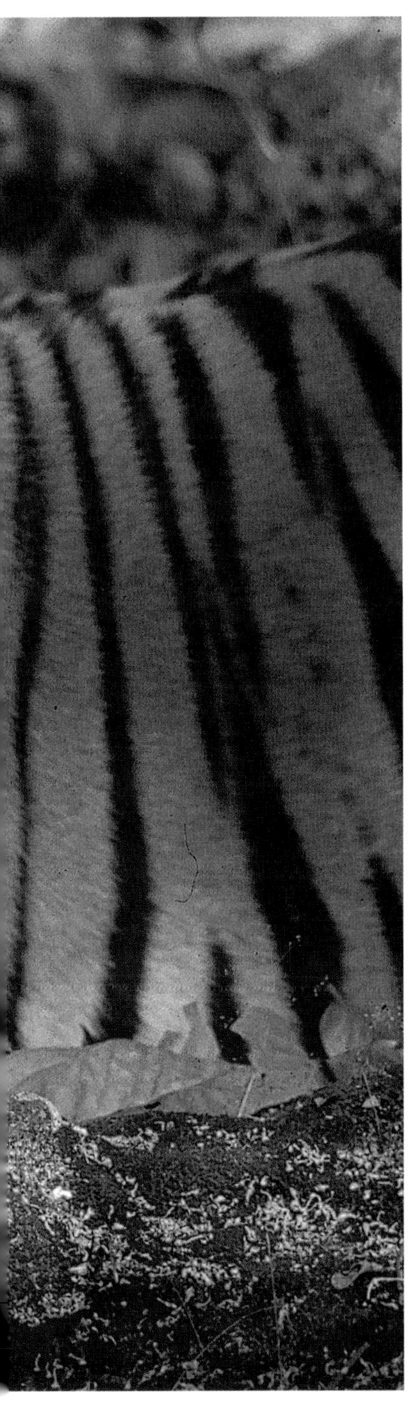

smaller animals with a final spring and tremendous blow of the paw or lethal bite to the nape of the neck. The momentum of the sudden attack rolls the prey over and generally the neck is twisted in the opposite direction resulting in neck dislocation and instantaneous death. The crushing power of the jaw is enormous and sometimes the bite alone may fracture the skull or crush the vertebrae. For larger prey a throat attack is preferred; the head is pinned down and strangulation hold kept till life ebbs away. The tiger's sharp retractable claws help to hold on to prey. A single powerful blow of the paw often kills small species like peafowl or porcupine. Porcupine quills broken inside the paw are often the cause of a tiger turning man-eater, since the sores severely restrict it in catching normal prey.

Left: *Fully grown Balram resenting our close approach.*

Below: *Balram growls as he cools himself near the Charanganga stream.*

Left: *Balram making a deer-kill. He has just rushed a chital stag and has caught its throat.*

Bottom Left: *An injured Banka, resting on Dodua hills on 16 February 1990. He had a fight in the night over a kill with a younger tiger, later named Charger. Banka was injured in his front leg–one wound was quite large and there were a number of smaller injuries. He recovered but became lame. He continued in the territory till 6 February 1992, but then was seen no more. Charger became the dominant tiger of Bandhavgarh and sired the next four litters of Sita.*

Right: *This is Charger, who injured Banka the territorial tiger of Bandhavgarh. He was about six to seven years old in 1990 and was noted for his aggression. There was a time when he was considered almost a terror and even the veteran mahouts gave him a wide berth. Charger used to viciously charge any vehicle or the forest elephants which intruded into his area. Except for a brief period when another tiger called Bhagora (the fleer) tried to take over his territory, he remained the dominant tiger of the tourist zone for ten long years. He finally died of old age on 29 September 2000, in an enclosure erected for his welfare by the Park authorities.*

It generally makes one large kill every seven or eight days and can eat up to 18 kg (40 lb) or more of meat in a single sitting. An average prey such as spotted deer may be finished in two or three days, or even at the first sitting itself if the tiger has been without food for many days. It is estimated that a tiger needs about 50 to 60 deer in a year for its sustenance. A tigress with two growing cubs has to kill more to feed the cubs. The prey species available in the territory should be at least 350 in number per tiger, to ensure that the prey population is not adversely affected by the predation.

The tiger almost always starts feeding at the rump, after removing the skin with its carnassials and after clawing out the rumen and the intestines. After the first feed, the kill is dragged into cover and hidden with grass, foliage or stones to avoid detection by scavengers like jackal, hyena, vulture or crow. The tiger then goes to drink at the nearest waterhole and returns to rest not far from the kill to keep watch.

Tiger Territory

The tiger is a territorial animal of solitary habits and does not share its territory with others of the same species. Its home range covers about 128 sq km (50 sq miles) or more, depending upon the habitat area and the prey-density: the smaller the prey-density, the bigger the territory is. Overlap of range

Right: *The fourth litter of Sita, sired by Charger, comprised two cubs, Mohini and a blind cub with paralysed hind legs. They were born in February 1994. The handicapped cub died, but Mohini, on attaining adulthood, moved over to Bhadrashila, Mahaman, and Thondhi and Jhorjhura areas of the Park. She gave birth in 1997 to three male cubs. One male, called B1, has moved to the fringes of the Park and the other, called B2, took over the domain of Charger after his death. The third cub, B3, stayed with Mohini but later moved to Gonhdi and Raj Behra areas of the Park. The picture shows the 15 to 16-months-old B1, standing over a rock in April 1998.*

between adults of the same sex is not tolerated for reasons of minimum prey base and water requirement. A male's territory, however, overlaps the range of two or three females.

The adult regularly patrols its territory marking the boundary by scratching tree trunks, spraying a mixture of urine scented with a secretion from anal glands on bushes, trees and rocks, and scraping the ground and depositing its feces at conspicuous places along its trail. This communication system warns the transients seeking new territories to keep off and avoid confrontation. The female has a much smaller individual range, usually about 10 to 12 sq km (4 to 5 sq miles) within the home range of the tiger. The territory of a Siberian tiger could cover as much as 518 to 5180 sq km (200 to 2000 sq miles) or even more. The tiger occupies the same territory throughout its life, unless forced out by a more powerful rival or other circumstances like food or water scarcity.

Life Cycle

There is no particular season for the female to come into oestrus. Once in oestrus, the male locates the tigress from her distinctive scent markings that leave a trail advertising her condition. She roars persistently and her haunting, low, rolling moans are carried over long distances and attract many males. The ultimate winner generally is the territorial tiger. Mating spreads over five to six days. The male then leaves, and the female is completely on her own during the gestation period of 102 to 105 days and in rearing the cubs, the male takes no interest. She selects a secluded place for giving birth such as a cave, dense vegetation, over-hanging

“She roars persistently and her haunting, low, rolling moans are carried over long distances and attract many males.”

Left: *B2 pulling down the bamboo.*

Right: *Mohini's cub, B2, drinking after feeding on a chital kill, below Thondhi hills in March 1998.*

rock or hollow of a tree, safe from flood or other jungle predators like jackal, hyena, wild dog or even python.

The litter is between one and seven cubs, although the average generally comprises three to five cubs. The cubs are born blind and the eyes open after about a week. The tigress has to leave the young after a few days, driven by hunger, and this is the time when the cubs are most vulnerable from

other predators, which come snooping if the tigress is not around. She generally hunts in the night, not going too far, and spends the day suckling the young, and guarding them. If she feels that the nursery has been discovered, immediate action is taken to shift the cubs to another safe place by carrying them between her teeth holding the loose skin on their necks and part of the head. There is a high mortality rate and generally only two to three cubs survive into the second year.

> "The life of a male tiger in the wild is about 12 to 15 years, though there is a record of a tiger in a zoo surviving up to 26 years."

The cubs are suckled for about six months and then they accompany their mother to feed on the kill. After about two months, however, the mother starts them up on small pieces of meat which she brings from her kills. The cubs are completely dependent on their mother until they are about 18 months old, though they start hunting animals like chital deer at about 15 months of age. At this point the male cub is larger in size than the mother; the female cub is of the same size.

Right: *B1 had killed a wild boar the previous night and taken the kill inside a cave. He had cut off the head and started to feed from the neck. This was rather unusual, since tigers almost always start feeding from the rump. It was early morning at about 7 am, on 6 April 1999.*

Above: *Mohini the mother of B1, came to the cave at about 8 am, but the son did not allow her to share the kill.*

Overleaf: *Mohini kept on waiting till the evening, then left to make her own kill. A mother always allows cubs to feed first and eats only after the cubs have gorged themselves.*

The cubs remain with the mother until they are about 24 months old. Once the tigress feels that they have acquired adequate proficiency in catching small herbivores, she starts leaving them to their own devices for increasingly longer periods–even up to two or three days or more–but does not move too far away. This is an important part of their training to lead independent lives. This is also the beginning of the breaking-up process and loosening of the close social and emotional bond, which precedes their dispersal to their own permanent niche. Between the ages of 20 to 24 months the cubs move away, sometimes after some prodding from their

mother. The female cub may remain with the mother for an additional four to six months, honing its hunting skills.

The tigress is again alone after about two and a half years. She now comes into oestrus and is visited by the resident tiger and another cycle of motherhood starts. A female may raise four to five litters in her reproductive life.

The life of a male tiger in the wild is about 12 to 15 years, though there is a record of a tiger in a zoo surviving up to 26 years. In the wild there is fierce competition for food, mate and territory and there are transient tigers always in search of a permanent niche. A fight sometimes ensues, and one of the combatants gets injured or dies.

Left: *It was learnt that one of the tigresses from the sixth litter of Sita and Charger had replaced Sita after her disappearance, and that she was with two eight-month-old cubs sired by B2. While searching the foothills of the Bandhavgarh hills, the two cubs were seen on a small sal tree and a number of pictures were taken. The mother had gone for a kill and the cubs were in a tree to protect themselves from co-predators.*

Below: *Close up of a tiger*

The Bengal Tiger

The Bengal Tiger, *Panthera tigris tigris (P.t. tigris),* is distributed through the humid forests and grasslands of India, southern Nepal, Bhutan, Bangladesh and western Myanmar (Burma). At the turn of the twentieth century, there were about 40,000 tigers spread all over the country. During the Second World War, its habitat came under considerable pressure due to extensive logging operations and army training in guerrilla warfare in the forests. After the country's independence in 1947, the forests and their denizens became public property and indiscriminate destruction of habitat and wildlife became widespread, with guns freely available. By 1971, the population had come down to only about 1800 tigers. Indian Prime Minister Indira Gandhi took a personal interest and, with support of many non-government organisations such as the

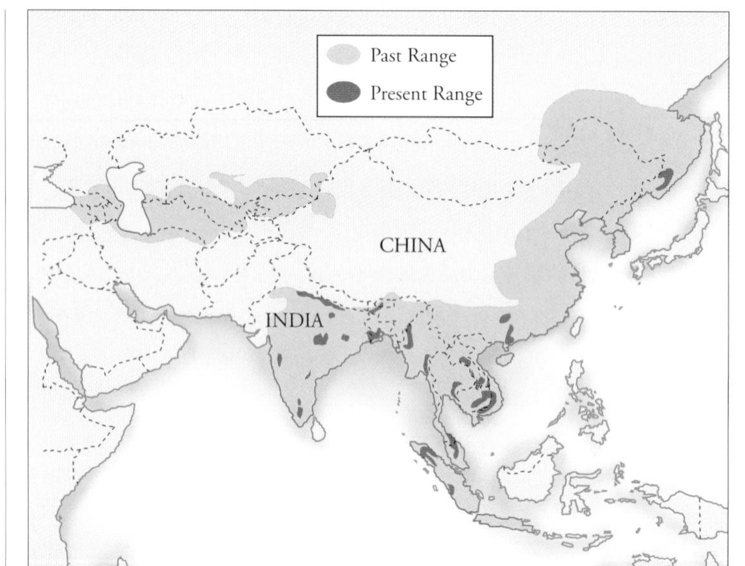

Left: *Map illustrating tiger distribution both past and present.*

World Wide Fund For Nature, Project Tiger was launched focusing on strict conservation measures. There was a steady improvement in population till the 1980s, and numbers increased to nearer 4500 individuals. Then the poaching pressure began and there was a sudden fall in numbers. In the last official census in 1997, the number was estimated to be 3508.

The coat of the Bengal tiger is usually fawn to deep orangish-red with a white underside and almost black transverse stripes. The average length of the male Bengal tiger is about 2.9 metres (9.5 feet) from head to tail and weighs about 270 kg (480 lb). It is next in size to the Siberian subspecies. The female is smaller in size and on average measures around 2.5 metres (8 feet) and weighs approximately 136 Kg (300 lb).

The Bengal tiger accounts for about sixty per cent of the five subspecies, that survive today. The population is distributed over six countries: India, Bangladesh, Nepal, Bhutan, China and Mynamar.

Left: *On 29 March 1989, we heard that four tigers were feeding on a deer kill in Ladiware forest near the Ghangar nullah. We hurried inside the forest with the mahout Lakhan Singh, but when we located the deer kill it was almost completely eaten. On searching the area, we saw a large tigress with two about nine-month-old cubs. Not too far away, we saw the fourth tiger, about four years old, sitting on a 10 metre (30 feet) high rock.*

Country	**Minimum**	**Maximum**
India	2500	3000-3508*
Bangladesh	300	460
Nepal	150	250
Bhutan	80	240
China	30	35
Mynamar	Not known	
Total	3060	3985-4493

*Census figure of 1997

Once Bengal tiger in good number were living in Myanmar. But militancy and poaching have taken their toll and the present number is not known. The population is generally estimated from the identification of pugmarks, because

Left: *This is Choti Mada (younger female), daughter of Badi Mada (elder female), a well known tigress of Chubri (wet land) of Kanha, who raised many litters in the Park. Choti Mada was resting in the meadow when our elephant happened to approach too close. She snarled viciously and we withdrew.*

Right: *A tiger of Kanha*

“However by the late 1980s, the decreased visibility of tigers became noticeable. Indeed it became alarming.”

photographing individual tigers on a scale necessary for a census is not feasible for logistical and financial reasons. However the pugmark method is susceptible to human error and manipulation. A field biologist once presented 35 pugmarks to different experts, who extrapolated this to a tiger population of six to 23. In fact, he claimed, the pugmarks were of only four zoo tigers. It is also pertinent to bear in mind that the official estimates of tiger populations tend to be on the higher side, which is hardly surprising given the fact that the performance of forest officials is evaluated by the wildlife growth in their preserves. On the other hand, I have

Right: *A tiger of Kanha coming down the hill in late afternoon. Generally tigers retire in the morning to their caves or shady spots on the surrounding hills, after spending the night hunting for prey in the meadow.*

Left: *Another progeny of Badi Mada tigress comes to drink at Choti Chuhri in Kanha.*

found during my interactions with the local tribal population, elephant mahouts and forest guards that they are more intimately aware of the number of tigers in their areas. The composition of tiger groups and their movements are of significant interest to them, and their whole sphere of activity often overlaps with that of the tiger. Hence their estimates of numbers can be surprisingly precise, though they are generally lower than the official estimates. It is felt that their input should also be taken into account in arriving at a more accurate census figure. Otherwise there will continue to be more tigers on paper than in the wild!

India: Nearly eighty percent of the Bengal tiger population is concentrated in India. Probably the species has had more chance of survival here for a longer period, than in any other country, because of greater vigilance, a stronger conservation movement and global attention focused on the plight of Bengal tiger. There was a rapid decrease in its population from 1947 to 1970, because of heavy destruction of tiger habitat to facilitate large development projects such as hydroelectric dams, mining, agriculture and human resettlement. The first official census in 1972 recorded the population of tiger to be about 1800 in the wild - down from about 4000 in 1947. This fall caused a worldwide concern about the future of this magnificent animal and with the assistance of the World Wide Fund For Nature, Project Tiger was launched in 1973. The initial nine sites for the Project have since been extended to cover 23 sites, spread over 14 States and covering an area of about 30,046 sq km (11,400 sq miles). On account of the total protection provid-

Above: *This seven-month-old male cub had very unusual markings on his front legs.*

Left: *A nearly three-year-old tiger, squatting with a straw in mouth. He was in a playful mood in a forest patch near Sanduk Khol road in Kisli range.*

A tigress known as 'Sonapani tigress' in Kanha, sitting under a banyan tree at about 9:30 am on April 2001. She had three 18-month-old cubs, two females and one male.

ed to the tiger and its habitat, and because of improved protected area management, the population was said to have increased to 4334 by the year 1989. Even if the official figure was contested, there was little doubt that the tiger population had significantly increased after the launch of Project Tiger.

However, by the late 1980s, the decreased visibility of tigers became noticeable. Indeed it became alarming. In the Ranthambhore Park alone, where in 1985-86 it was not very unusual to see four to nine tigers on a single outing, even one sighting became an event. There were widespread rumours about large scale poaching by organised mafia. Largely due to the efforts of non-government organisations, such as TRAFFIC and individuals like Belinda Wright of the Wildlife Protection Society of India, tiger poaching for gain was exposed. Many of the poachers and traders were arrested and a large quantity of tiger bones, skin and body parts was confiscated. The penalty for tiger poaching in India is a fine of Rs. 5000 (£166) and jail sentence of one to six years. Unfortunately the laws are not rigorously enforced and the cases drag on for months. In the meantime the culprits are released on bail and sometimes continue with their nefarious activities. Indeed, over the years, only very few people have been convicted for tiger poaching in India. The poachers use poison, guns, steel traps and electrocution by tapping power from overhead cables and laying down the wires on tracks frequented by tigers.

> **“The penalty for tiger poaching in India is a fine for Rs. 5000 (£166) and a jail sentence of one to six years.”**

The people living on the fringes of tiger reserves are generally very poor and have partially subsisted for hundreds of years on minor forest produce, while their livestock has always grazed in the forests. With the formation of parks and

Right: *A tiger on the prowl. When not stalking, tigers move at a steady pace of, say, 5 to 8 kph (3.5 to 5 mph). When moving in a purposeful manner, as when stalking, the hind leg is placed exactly over the spot vacated by the front foot to minimize the chance of any noise.*

Below Right: *This tiger was out hunting in Kisli forests during a summer morning of 2001. A wild boar was seen approaching and the tiger crouched low in the grass. When the boar was hardly 12 metres (36 feet) from the tiger, a langur on the tree gave alarm and the boar immediately turned and scurried away. The frustrated tiger looks up at the langur angrily.*

Left: *Face of a tiger - close-up.*

Right: *This picture of a tigress called 'Noon' was taken on March 17 1987 at Ranthambhore National Park. In the morning she made a sambar kill and dragged it into some long khus grass near a narrow stream which provided the overflow of water between two nearby lakes Rajbagh and Padam Talao. The next two days we spent observing the tigress and her two 10-month-old cubs feeding, drinking and interacting with each other. Here Noon relaxes after a good feed.*

reserves, access was denied to them and they felt deprived of what they thought was their right. Their cattle were sometimes taken by the tiger provoking a lot of hostility. Belatedly the Government, with the assistance of WWF's Tiger Conservation Project, has introduced a Cattle Compensation Programme for the livestock lost by villagers due to predation. An India Eco Development Project was conceived in June 1994 and became operational around the end of 1997. This project plans to involve the villagers around the tiger parks in the conservation of the habitat, by assisting them to lessen their dependence on the forest. They are encouraged

to raise fast-growing fuel woods, and plant fodder plantations to meet their requirements.

Tiger poaching has decreased in the primary tiger areas of Madhya Pradesh and Rajasthan. However the poachers seem to have shifted their activities to new areas that have so far been considered immune from poaching, such as Corbett National Park. It has been reported recently that five tigers have fallen victim to poachers in less than a month in the Corbett Park. The rise of militancy in Assam and Andhra Pradesh has added another dimension to the problem, as these elements sometimes take refuge in wildlife parks and raise funds by resorting to poaching. Bittu Sahgal, a member of the Indian Wildlife Board and editor of the well known magazine, *Sanctuary Asia,* estimates that one tiger is being lost in India per day and that the tiger population may reach a figure lower than required for long term survival within a decade if measures are not taken immediately to secure the safety of the tigers left in the wild.

Far Left: *A tigress protests close approach. On 21 January 1988, while approaching the Bhakola range of Ranthambhore at about 9 am, we saw from a distance a tigress, known as 'Bhakola tigress', killing a chital deer and dragging the kill into a dense patch. We returned after an hour or so and backed our Gypsy near the patch. The tigress emerged to protest and we retreated. She looked hungry and the kill was lying behind her. The Gypsy driver informed us that the tigress had two six-month-old cubs on a nearby hill. She will bring the cubs in the evening and feed only after the cubs have eaten.*

Above: *We came across the Bhakola tigress again next day. She seemed annoyed and walked towards us as if about to charge and we departed in haste.*

Right: *A tiger of Semli, Ranthambhore, stalking. Until 1989 one could see many tigers in a day in the Ranthambhore Park, but subsequently the tiger population decreased drastically due to organized poaching. It is surmised that between 1989 and 1992 alone, 18 tigers disappeared including Noon, Laxmi, the Bhakola tigress and their cubs. Their body parts were probably smuggled to China and the Far East. One poacher, Gopal Mogia, who was caught, confessed to having shot or poisoned about 12 tigers inside the Park. He was assisted by an organized gang with headquarters at Delhi. The number of poached tigers should be much more, according to local people. However, due to strict protection now provided, the tiger population has been on a come-back trail since 1995.*

Nepal: The tiger population in Nepal is mainly concentrated in three fragmented populations in the lowland areas. Chitwan and Parsa contain 45 or 50 tigers, the Royal Bardia National Park (RBNP) has 37 and just 14 resident tigers live in the Royal Sukla Phanta Wildlife Reserve with another two in a proposed extension area. The future of Bengal tiger in Nepal to an extent depends on the trans-border cooperation for the threats are similar. The breeding number of tigers in the isolated pockets seems to be too low for a long-term genetically viable population. The Government of Nepal is planning to extend the RBNP by including additional tiger habitat. The tiger population in Nepal has decreased by about 95 per cent in the last 100 years, due to habitat shrinkage, reduced prey base, poisoning, use of pipe guns and poaching for tiger parts. Being a contiguous country to China has only exacerbated the problem.

Bangladesh: About 360 to 460 tigers are officially said to exist in three protected areas in Bangladesh; the population is largely concentrated in the southwestern coastal part called Sundarbans. Sundarbans is a cluster of islands with an area of about 3600 sq kms (1406 sq miles), with the world's largest mangroves forests shared with India. Water transport is the only means of transport inside the forest. For some reason a high proportion of tigers in Sundarbans turn man-eaters, and in-depth research is needed to establish the reasons for this uncommon tiger behaviour. It could be the brackish water, low prey density and unauthorised honey and firewood collectors being mistaken as prey in the dense forest. It is not unusual to come across a tiger swimming across the streams and occasionally attacking boatmen or their passengers. The comparative inaccessibility of an area, where there are no roads or paths is, in a way, fortunate for the tiger. The fear of

a man-eater in Sundarbans also keeps humans at bay. The Bangladesh Government has plans to drill for oil in these pristine areas, through a Production Sharing Contract with Shell Oil Company and Cavin Energy. Only time will tell what effect this will have on the tiger habitat.

Bhutan: Bhutan, a mountainous country, still has 64 per cent forest cover and also a low human population density - both factors congenial to a safe tiger habitat. The easy money that tiger parts fetch, however, has led to increased poaching and

Left: *Cub playing with mother. We had unsuccessfully searched for the tigress and her cubs during the morning of January 1, 2000. Near Belkui Nullah we heard repeated alarm calls of deer at about 3:30 pm. and we saw the tigress coming at a distance beyond the dry nullah. She crossed the nullah and softly called "Aaooon", "Aaooon" many times. The three cubs, one by one, emerged from the patch and a very joyful scene followed. We later learnt that the tigress had killed a stray cow about a kilometre away on a plateau. The cubs must have sensed the ready food and for about 30 minutes played with each other and the mother. Here a cub sits on the mother and pulls at her face as she seems to say, "Stop it. It hurts".*

Right: *The tigress about to lick the paw of one of the cubs playfully.*

this keeps anti-poaching squads very busy, according to Karma Tshering of the Government of Bhutan. He feels that the local population, being highly dependent on their livestock, consider the tiger as a major predator and often kill it by poisoning or trapping. What happens to the tiger population by 2010 is dependent on the Government's sustained efforts in controlling threats such as poaching, introducing better management of the protected areas and involving the villagers in saving the wildlife. According to a recent tiger survey, the tiger population in Bhutan is 75 to 150, including

Overleaf: *Two cubs mock fighting.*

Above: *A tigress with her three grown-up cubs. The cubs remain with the mother till they are about two to two-and-a-half-years old and then they separate out to find their own territories. The female cub may continue to be with mother for a few more months.*

cubs and sub-adults, spread in five protected areas: Royal Manas National Park, Jigme Dorji National Park, Black Mountain National Park, Phipso Wildlife Sanctuary and Thrumsingla National Park– where recently a tiger was photographed at an altitude of nearly 3000 metres (10,000 feet). The Royal Manas National Park, which it shares with India, is the largest and richest among the protected areas of Bhutan. Although Bhutan has stringent legislation for wildlife protection, the enforcement is weak. Further, a number of Bodo and ULFA militants from Assam in India have their secret training camps in Bhutan and resort to poaching for purchase of arms.

A Grim Future

Just 10 decades ago there were around 100,000 tigers freely roaming the vast forests of central, northern and southeastern Asia. But today the population has dwindled to approximately 6000. This drastic reduction has not been because of any natural calamity or epidemic, but due to deliberate acts of Man. Of the eight subspecies of tiger, three–Caspian, Javan and Bali subspecies–are already extinct. The fourth–South Chinese –might also have disappeared by now.

The threats to the survival of the tiger are well known, researched and identified–fragmentation, degradation and loss of habitat, and prey base depletion, leading to man-tiger conflict. Added to this is the greatest threat of all–poaching by organised gangs for tiger bone and organs to feed the phenomenal demand for traditional Chinese medicines throughout the world. Though legal provisions for protecting the tiger have been in place for quite some time in all the tiger countries, their enforcement has been weak. Consequently the tiger has been driven to confined habitats and genetic threat to the species is very real.

Once the dodo was a very common bird on the Island of Mauritius, before it was shot and clubbed to extinction in 1681. The last Steller's cow was killed in Bering Island in 1768. The beautiful passenger pigeon was once estimated to number more than five billion in North America. It was massacred in large numbers by relentless hunters and the last passenger pigeon was shot on 24th March 1900 in Pike County, Ohio. The Indian pink-headed duck became extinct in 1940 and the last Indian Cheetah was shot in 1952. The list is long and depressing and unfortunately the tiger seems destined to be added.

It has been estimated that nearly 15 per cent of the earth's species may be extinct by the year 2020–all victims of man's short sightedness, cruelty and greed. Let us hope that the tiger, the magnificent and the most powerful species the world has ever seen, and the main instrument of Nature for maintaining balance in the forest ecosystem, will not get reduced to a mere item in the statistics of extinct species.

"Nature is ruthless, red in tooth and claw, as it has the very long-term aim of perpetuation of species."

THE CO-PREDATORS

PREDATION IS AN IMPORTANT INSTRUMENT of Nature in maintaining the ecological balance that is so essential for life processes. It is a symbiotic predator-prey relationship in which, in the long run, both the predator as well as the prey benefit. Predators remove the old, sick, slow or less wary animals from the herd, thus keeping the breeding stock strong. They are Nature's strong regulatory agents of natural selection, ensuring survival of the fittest. Predation also prevents the prey outgrowing the carrying capacity of an ecosystem, thus diminishing its ability to support life. To quote Volterra's principle, reduction of predators and prey by the same proportion results in faster recovery by prey than predators. There are always a smaller number of predators relative to the

Left: *Portrait of a predator; close up of an angry leopard.*

Left: *A leopard of Nagarhole.*

prey. Without human interference, in natural systems, predators and prey fluctuate in a dynamic balance. If the number of prey decreases, predators diminish accordingly, and vice versa. This balance prevents predators from becoming too many or prey too scarce. There can be time lags between the events and for some time the predator and prey population may oscillate, but ultimately the natural balance is achieved.

If one spends time in the jungles observing nature, it will be observed that the concepts of kindness, compassion and mercy are wholly human traits. Nature is ruthless, red in tooth and claw, as it has the very long-term aim of perpetuation of species. It enforces its laws inexorably to achieve its objective and concessions are never made. One may assume that the prey species that share the forest ecosystem with the predators lead a tense life. That is not so, because they accept the natural law of existence. I have, a few times, observed a herd of deer being attacked and one of them being killed. The herd ran away in panic but, after making sure that the predator had a prey and thus would not be hunting for some time, soon become busy again not too far away with its normal activities such as feeding, courting, sparring, and suckling the young. Once, in Kanha National Park, I saw a fawn being caught by a wild dog. The mother returned to observe the fawn being killed, then rejoined the rest of the herd and resumed grazing. It would not be long before it was in oestrus again and raised another family.

Life Support Systems

Nature's supreme aim, transcending all emotions, is to ensure continuation of life on earth by sustaining and reinforcing the essential life support systems, based primarily on nourishing air, water and soil. To achieve its objective, Nature, the Great Director, has allotted a role to all its creation. Sometimes we may guess what the aim is and sometimes we may be ignorant, but the role is there. The focus is always on achieving equilibrium between the harmonious coexistence of a community of organisms and its environment. It is we, Homo sapiens, who, intoxicated with technology, try to allot a role to ourselves independent of other organisms and disturb the delicate balance. But it is certain that our coming generations will have to suffer for our hubris. Nature bats last and is always the winner.

Crucial Balance

Let us start with the very important role of trees and forests in maintaining the crucial balance in Nature. The tree absorbs the carbon dioxide emitted by the growing population of man and other organisms and, with the energy of the sun, releases oxygen back into the atmosphere–a process essential for survival of life on earth. It helps to retain moisture and condense low clouds, thus increasing precipitation, and brings out underground water through transpiration. Forests also stem the wind velocity and prevent the soil from blowing away. It is primarily the tree that holds the good topsoil back from soil run-off in heavy rain. Nature desires more and more trees to grow, and herbivores, both mammals and birds, are allotted assisting roles to disperse seeds far and wide. Even the air is used for this purpose.

Natural cultivation

In the forests one finds wild boars digging earth with their snouts in search of tubers. In the process they loosen the topsoil, which becomes primed to receive seeds. If any seed falls into this 'ploughed patch' during its dispersal, and receives moisture, it germinates and a sapling springs up. The seed generally comes enveloped in the manure of animal drop-

Above: *A sun- dappled Leopard grooming.*

pings. The grass around it, however, will grow faster and could soon smother the sapling by depriving it of essential sunlight. The herbivores now play their role and start working as nature's cultivators, by trimming the grass without harming the sapling. If, however, they are left in the same patch for too long a period, overgrazing could ultimately lead to desertification, which Nature, of course, does not desire as it is against its life support system. It now sends a predator, such as a tiger, leopard or a pack of wild dogs. A herbivore, generally old, very young or one with low defenses, gets killed, driving the herd away to some other forest patch to start its cultivation activities again. The predator remains in the plot for a few days with the kill, thus permitting regeneration of grass.

As the plant grows, the leaves are attacked by insects and

Right: *A very large tiger about 10 years old.*

then the birds come to feed on them. The bird population is also kept under control by predators like raptors. So Nature distributes roles to all its creation to achieve its main aim of sustaining life on earth, by maintaining the delicate ecological balance. It operates in the background, very unobtrusively pulling the strings, with no one getting any wiser.

Some Observations

A.A. Dunbar Brander in his famous book, *Wild Animals In Central India,* records his experience of what happened once the tigers were shot out in a forest patch in Hoshangabad district of the then Central India. There was an outlying patch of forest in the district that always contained a few tigers when he visited the forest in 1906. Perhaps they sometimes lifted the livestock of the villagers and so were all eliminated. He visited this tract again in 1917, on one of his official tours as a forest officer. He found the surrounding villagers completely overrun with pig and nilgai and many fields had gone out of cultivation. He felt that to reintroduce a couple of tigers into that forest would be a great boon to the local people and he advocated: "extermination of tiger in such places should not be permitted." Although tigers do a great deal of damage, he observed, they have their role to perform in preserving the balance of nature.

> "The leopard will eat almost anything it can catch and overcome. Its food varies from small deer and antelope, to wild boar, monkey, porcupine, reptiles, peafowl, fish and crabs."

Sharon Woods Metro Park is one of the largest parks in the Metropolitan Park District of Columbus and Franklin County of Ohio. It is a very beautiful park covering 761 acres, with nearly three miles of nature trails meandering through woodland and meadows. I have been visiting this park every

Left: A close-up of a charging leopard.

alternate year since 1990 to enjoy its scenic landscapes, and also to photograph the friendly white tailed deer which were easily spotted throughout the park. They were introduced as a tourist attraction and in due course had multiplied in numbers from 190 in 1989 to 450 in 1993. During a visit in the summer of 1996, I was disappointed not to see them and made enquiries in the office of the Park District. I was told that the deer population had grown beyond the carrying capacity of the park and the deer had multiplied themselves "into plague proportions, gobbling up ornamental shrubs and ground plants. The forest area was over grazed and the vegetation cover was in grave danger. There was impact even on the nutritional health of the deer herd itself and on other animal species in the park. The park lost 250 species of plants and the overpopulation impacted food/cover for other species of insects, birds and mammals." The park authorities tried relocating the deer elsewhere but did not find it feasible. It took them more than six months to organise media and popular support, but culling was then carried out and only about 36 deer were left inside the park by the year 2000. To release a few predators would have probably taken care of the problem, but the park was in the centre of the town and was frequented by a large number of visitors. It appeared to me that the park authorities had merely postponed the problem, which was sure to confront them again after a few years, so that they will have to resort to regular culling.

Nature ensures harmony and dynamic balance in each ecosystem. If there is human interference and if one element alone is transplanted into another habitat without the balancing organisms which have co-evolved, ecological complications are likely to arise. This has been learnt the hard way by many countries, which imported exotic organisms for what they thought were beneficial reasons.

Co-Predators

Nature has a predator for every species, depending upon its size and habitat. If there is no natural predator for a species and its population grows beyond the carrying capacity of the ecosystem, Nature generally makes sure that the species preys, on each other, during competition for food or mates. The tiger takes care of most of the larger prey species. It has a lifespan of over twenty years in a zoo, but in the wild normally it does not survive beyond 12 to 15 years. It is then usually killed or injured in a fight with a younger and stronger tiger, which wants to take over its territory.

Generally there are many levels of operation of predators, and competition, wherever possible, is avoided. The leopard is a co-predator with the tiger for deer and smaller mammals, but it avoids any confrontation with the tiger. The wild dog is a feared predator, which even a tiger avoids. It makes up for its comparatively smaller size by hunting in packs and its ability to sustain pursuit over long distances. The lion lives in its own special niche in the Gir forest and there is little possibility of any interaction between the lion and the tiger. There are other co-predators in the forest, such as hyena, jackal, wildcat and mongoose, which share the forest ecosystem with the tiger. Himalayan bear often kill hangul fawns in spring, after coming out of winter hibernation–though its normal food is fruit, beehive, termite and even carcass.

"The leopard is, probably, the most adaptable of all the big cats and is known to thrive from snowline to sea level, from rain forest to arid desert, from broken rocky outcrops to rural or semi-urban areas."

Further predators in the wild are the fox, civet cat, and the reptiles–including the crocodile, which is the only large aquatic predator in the tiger habitat. Generally a wolf confines

Right: *A close up of the stunning face of a leopard.*

Right: *Wild dog relaxing after a feed. Rudyard Kipling referred to the wild dog as 'red peril' in his well-known* The Jungle Book. *He gave a very unsympathetic portrayal reflecting the age-old prejudice against the species.*

itself to open country, but it is sometimes found on the outskirts of a forest, preying on mammals such as blackbuck and chinkara. Hyena, jackal, vulture and some birds such as the tree-pie and crow, are the camp followers of the tiger feeding on the half eaten kills and assisting in keeping the environment clean.

The Spider is also a co-predator in the forest eco-system, effectively controlling the population of insects. It is very interesting to observe a spider in its orb. It rests motionlessly in its corner for long periods; but attacks with extraordinary agility, once a prey is caught in the web. It reminds me of the tiger, which also rests under some cover for most of the time, conserving the energy that will be required for the few moments of the actual charge and killing of the prey, when it becomes aggression personified.

Man, with his access to powerful weapons, deludes himself that he is the ultimate predator on earth. But Nature has not forgotten him and has devised a predator for him also. It has, however, chosen the smallest of all predators–so small that it is invisible to the naked eye–to prick man's ego and lay him low. This predator is the bacterium.

Though most bacteria are extremely useful for continuing life, there are some that, along with a still smaller microorganism the virus, prey on man. Even after death, bacteria continue to work on him, decomposing him into the basic elements of air, water and earth – man's main constituents. They decompose even the bones and the nutrients are recycled back into the earth. In fact the bacterium is the most powerful agent of nature, without which there can be no life.

The Co-predator Species

Leopard, *Panthera pardus:* The leopard is a sleek and beautiful animal, typically of golden tawny coat patterned with close-set black rosettes. The belly is clean white. Its whiskers are long and it has extra long hairs in the eyebrows, which protect the eyes while it is moving through thickets in the night. It is, probably, the most adaptable of all the big cats and is known to thrive from snowline to sea level, from rain forest to arid desert, from broken rocky outcrops to rural or semi-urban areas. In view of its survival ability in very diverse eco-systems, with considerably varying weather and prey availability, over time a variation in appearance and behaviour has occurred and many sub-species are said to exist. Variation in colour of the coat has been the chief basis for the description of the sub-species. Rainforest leopard is generally a deep gold colour, the animals of arid regions are pale cream to yellow-brown, while the leopard inhabiting the Himalayas are much lighter in colour with small, thick-rimmed rosettes.

The variation of colour is Nature's scheme to provide suitable camouflage allowing a better chance of survival to both the predators and the prey species. If the predator is easily spotted, it diminishes its chances of finding food.

Sometimes, in mostly humid forest habitats, black-coloured leopard is found. This is, however, not a sub-species, but merely a case of melanism. There are records of a litter having both normal as well as black cubs. In all my wanderings in Indian forests over the last two and a half decades, I have seen a black leopard only once in the Manas National Park on the border of Assam and Bhutan. They are said to be common in the Southern high rainfall areas of the Western Ghats. Dunbar Brander in 1913 once saw a leopard at Melghat in the then Central Provinces, which was intermediate in tint between a black leopard and a normal leopard. J.C. Daniel in his book, *The Leopard In India,* quotes shikaris of early last century who shot black leopards in the then Sind province and Gujarat. There is a widespread belief that there are two distinct species called leopard and panther, the panther being much larger. This controversy needs to be buried. It is now generally agreed that there was no difference and that both terms referred to the same animal. The fact seems to be that the forest-living leopard are of large size and sometimes may even be mistaken in the night for a tiger. The leopard near villages are much smaller and the leopard frequenting both villages and forests may be of intermediate size.

Dunbar Brander, who shot a large number of leopards, has recorded that forest living large leopard might be anything from 2.18 metres (7 feet 2 inches) up to 2.36 metres (7 feet 9 inches) in length and weigh on an average up to 68 kg (152 lb). The intermediate size might measure about 2.03 metres (6 feet 8 inches) and weigh 110 lb. The size of an ordinary adult leopard varied from 1.62 metres (5 feet. 4 inches)

Right: *After the charge the leopard kills prey by biting through the neck and holding on till the victim dies of strangulation.*

Overleaf: *A seated leopard during the heat of the day.*

Right: *An old leopard standing in the forest. It has to be extremely careful of tiger and even wild dogs, which do not hesitate to prey upon it.*

to 2.13 metres (7 feet) in length and from 27 kg to 59 kg (60 lb to 130 lb) in weight. The female is much smaller in length and weight, 30 cm (1 foot) less in length and about 34 kg (75 lb) less in weight. The largest animal shot by the Maharajah of Nepal is reported to be 2.76 metres (9 feet 1 inch) in length. It may not be fair to compare the measurements given by different shikaris unless the method of measurement is known. Brander writes that the size depends on whether the animal was gorged or not when weighed. The total length of a leopard often conveys a wrong impression as to its size, since the length of the tail bears little or no relation to the size of the body. Brander had seen some diminutive leopards with immense tails, and again a large beast with a short tail.

The leopard will eat almost anything it can catch and overcome. Its food varies from small deer and antelope, to wild boar, monkey, porcupine, reptiles, peafowl, fish and crabs. Those living near human habitation prey upon village dogs and livestock. Unlike the tiger, the leopard can be a wasteful feeder and kills more than it needs. It is very elusive and difficult to spot, since leopard living near villages are completely nocturnal in habit. In the forest, it has to be extremely careful of tiger and even wild dogs, which do not hesitate to prey upon it. It often carries its prey–even as large as a chital–up a tree and stores it there to keep it safe from other predators or scavengers. The leopard kills its prey by biting through the neck and holding on till the victim dies of strangulation. The 'village' leopard not only kills stray dogs but will even carry away chained dogs. The rare animal, that which turns man-eater, becomes a real terror, since living close to man, it is acquainted with man's habits and is not afraid to enter homes to pick up children and even adults, especially women. Because it is a very cunning animal, a man-eating leopard is much more difficult to kill than a man-

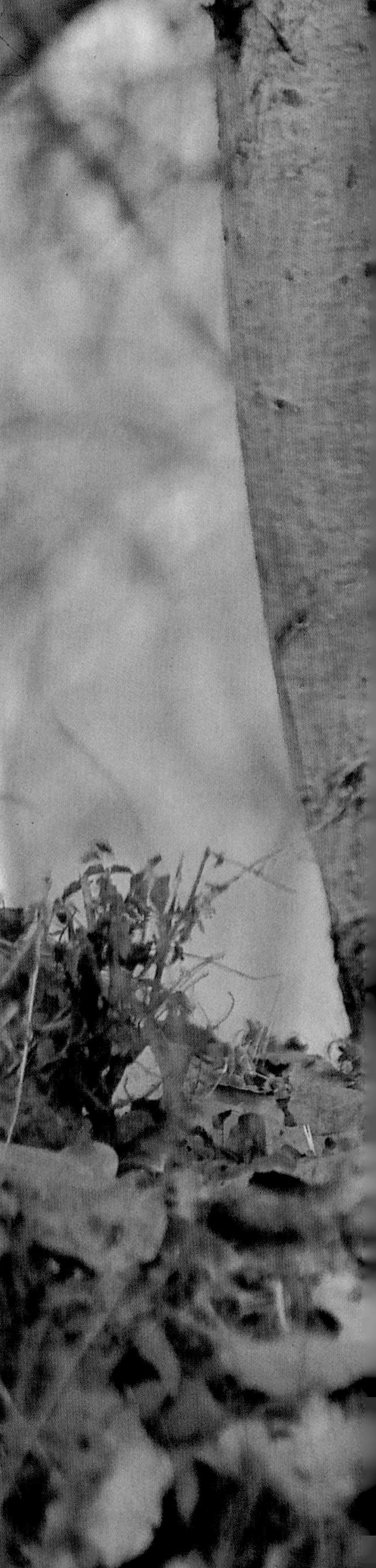

Left: *Wild dog pair feeding on a fawn.*

eating tiger. The man-eating leopard of Rudraprayag, which Jim Corbett eliminated after a sustained hunt lasting for more than a year, had killed 125 humans between 9 June 1918 and 14 April 1926. "I do know that the figure given is not correct," Corbett writes, "some kills which took place while I was on the ground have not been shown in the records."

The leopard makes a sawing vocalization–"haw-a-haw-a-haw-a-haw-a-haw"–resembling a piece of wood being sawn. There is no particular breeding season, but Brander observed more cubs being born in April than at any other time. The leopard is not as solitary as the tiger and the male remains with the female throughout the gestation period of about three months. Two to four cubs are born at a time. They are born blind and the spots are indistinct. The leopard can live as long as 21 years in captivity and up to about 12 in the wild.

Apart from man, its natural predators are tiger, wild dog and hyena. There are also known instances of a leopard being killed by a python or a crocodile. The main threat to its survival came from the international fur trade but has now received full protection internationally. At one time, a leopard skin coat could sell for \$20,000 to \$25,000 and it was estimated that the lifetime breeding effort of a pair of leopards went to make one fur coat!

Wild Dog or Dhole, *Cuon alpinus:* Rudyard Kipling referred to the wild dog as 'red peril' in his well-known *The Jungle Book*. He gave a very unsympathetic portrayal, reflecting the age-old prejudice against the species. In the old 'Shikar' days, the so-called sportsmen considered it as a competitor that got in the way of their sport of collecting 'record heads' of other forest wildlife. They branded it as a wanton and cruel killer, which deserved to be shot, poisoned or trapped. Its role, however, of maintaining the ecological balance and complementing other predators, like the tiger and leopard, is viewed more rationally now. Nature has a system of limiting the population of a species over a period appropriate to the health of an ecosystem. Once a peak is attained, rapid decline is brought about by disease or shortage of food. In India, R.C. Morris records, when wild dogs unduly increased in number in the Billigirirangan Hills of Karnataka, they developed virulent distemper and rabies, which reduced their population significantly.

The wild dog resembles the domestic Alsatian dog, with shorter legs and an unusually thick muzzle. Its ears are more rounded and the tail is bushy. The body length of an average adult is about 90 cm (35 inches), tail length 40 to 45 cm (16 to 18 inches) and height at the shoulder about 50 cm (20 inches). It has only four molars on the lower jaw, compared to six

in domestic dogs. The female has 12 to 14 teats to suckle its larger litter, unlike other members of the canidae family, which have only 10. The coat is of a distinctive red colour, shading into yellow or dirty white on the underside. The ears are pricked like an Alsatian and the tail has a bushy tuft of black hairs some 13 to 15 cm (5 to 6 inches) long at the end. The wild dog is found in scrub and dense forests up to 3000 metres (9840 feet) altitude, throughout Southeast Asia from eastern China to India, Myanmar, Malaysia and the islands of Java and Sumatra. In the last five decades, however, there has been extensive habitat loss within this region and probably the best remaining population is to be found in central and southern India. There are three subspecies in India viz., *C. .a. dukhunensis,* found south of River Ganga, *C. a. primaevus,* in Uttaranchal, Nepal Sikkim and Bhutan and, *C. a. laniger,* in Ladakh and northern Kashmir. Now only the subspecies in Central and Southern India are found and the others are either extinct or on the verge of extinction.

Left: *Wild dog at Bandipur. Wild dogs are highly social and cooperative animals. They live in organised packs ranging from 5 to 12 individuals.*

“Nature has a system of limiting the population of a species over a period appropriate to the health of an ecosystem.”

Wild dogs are highly social and cooperative animals. They live in organised packs ranging from 5 to 12 individuals. Occasionally larger groups of up to 40 animals have been spotted, but probably such assemblages comprise of neighbouring packs cooperating to hunt larger prey. The packs are territorial and there are more males than females in a pack. Wild dogs are diurnal in habit and hunting is normally done either in the early morning or in the late afternoon. In thick cover, a prey is selected and first followed by scent then pursued by sight. Once the prey is flushed out, it is chased by the pack maintaining a steady trot or galloping gait for a very long distance, till the prey is tired out and cornered. It is then attacked from all sides and is in no time disembowelled and killed. In fact, the dogs start feeding even before the prey is dead. It does not kill by strangulation–like the tiger or leopard–which takes longer to ebb the life; two or three dogs seldom take more than a couple of minutes to kill an adult chital of 50 kg. (110 lb). They do not compete by fighting with each other, but by being faster in gulping down chunks of food. A.J.T. Johnsingh of the Wildlife Institute of India, who has researched the species in depth, writes that a wild dog can gulp down 4 kg (8.8 lb) of meat in 60 seconds. If water is near, it will leave the kill for a few quick drinks; if at a distance it will race to the waterhole immediately after the meal. It is not afraid to enter water and likes to sit in shallow water even in the cold season. For its size, the wild dog can jump to an astonishing height of at least 2.3 metres (7.5 feet). It is an utterly fearless animal and there are many recorded incidents of a pack of wild dogs killing a leopard and even a tiger, though losing a few members in the process. It communicates by a series of vocal calls, including yelping, growling, howling or a peculiar whistling sound to assemble a dispersed pack.

Wild dogs reach sexual maturity at about one year of age. Whelping occurs between November and April and the gestation period is believed to be about 60 days. A cave, a sheltering rock or a disused burrow is chosen for the nursery and about 8 pups are born at a time, but not all will survive. The pups are fed with regurgitated meat after about three weeks and they leave the nursery after 70 to 80 days. The pack continues to take care of them by feeding them, by providing escorts, and allowing them priority of access at kills. At five months, Johnsingh records, pups actively follow the pack and at eight months, they participate in kills of even large prey such as sambar deer.

Indian Wolf, *Canis lupus pallipes:* The Indian wolf probably entered India from the desert areas of the Middle East and settled in open scrub lands rather than moist forest. It could not penetrate the dense forests because of competition from tiger, leopard and wild dog. The Indian wolf is smaller than its larger cousins that inhabit the tundra and boreal forest zones of North America and Eurasia. Those found in the barren uplands of Himalayan regions, like Gilgit, Ladakh, Kashmir or Tibet, are also the larger subspecies. The current range of the Indian wolf according to Dr. Yadvendra Jhala of the Wildlife Institute of India, extends from Gujarat and parts of Rajasthan in the west, to Bihar in the east, and south down the middle of India towards Madras and Karnataka. Presence of the the wolf in northern and eastern regions remains uncertain. It is also found in east Uttar Pradesh, from where cases of child lifting are reported from time to time. In forests where smaller antelopes like chinkara, blackbuck or chausingha are present, the wolf is sometimes found living on the outskirts of the forests to avoid tiger and leopard.

> "The Indian wolf is smaller than its larger cousins inhabiting the tundra and boreal forest zones of North America and Eurasia."

The height of the Indian wolf at the shoulders is 65 to 75 cm (26 in to 30 in); body length 90 to 105 cm (36 to 42 in) and the tail is about 35 to 40 cm (14 to 16 in) long. An adult male may weigh 18 to 27 kg (40 to 60 lb) compared to its larger cousin, which typically weighs 40 to 45 kg (90 to 100 lb). The male is usually fifteen per cent larger than females. The tracks of the Indian subspecies measured at 9.9 cm x 6.5cm (3 3/4 in x 2 in), smaller compared to their more northern counterparts. In general, the Indian wolves have a sandy fawn coat stippled with black. The Himalayan race may have a black to blackish coat. In captivity, it has been known to live for 15 years.

In the Indian desert, the wolves live in burrows dug in the sand dunes. In grassland, they remain above the ground lying up in the grass or patches of scrub and thorn forests. They hunt by day or night, but mostly by night. Their diet is diverse ranging from deer, antelope, gazelle, to goat, sheep and even rodents–whatever they can capture. They generally live in family packs from four to seven members, though packs with much larger numbers have been reported. These large packs are temporary and soon break up into smaller packs. Wolves are territorial and the size of the territory may vary from 60 sq km (25 sq miles) to much bigger areas, depending on availability of prey and the number of wolves that can exist within a pack without any conflict. Each wolf pack has a hierarchy, with a dominant male and a female wolf, called the alpha pair. The alpha wolves have the right to mate and eat first. Vocalization such as howling is a call to collect the pack together before a hunt. The Indian wolf preys not by chase but generally by ambush. It hunts in pairs, but for bigger prey resorts to cooperative hunting.

The main breeding season for the the Indian wolf is at the end of the rains, so the majority of cubs are dropped in December. The Himalayan race breed later and cubs are born in the spring or early summer. The gestation period is 60 to 68 days and females breed only once a year. Three to nine whelps are born blind in an underground den and are weaned in 5 to 8 weeks. Both the parents take care of the pups and bring food, which is regurgitated in front of them.

The Indian wolf has been in an unenviable situation. It cannot escape into the deep forest and so has to live on the outskirts or in open habitat, usually scrubland and hilly and unbroken areas. The cheetah once used to be its main com-

Right: *A wolf of Rollapadu. There are stories persisting in the villages for centuries of "wolf-children", where human children are brought up by a wolf pack. Such a belief was reflected in Rudyard Kipling's* "Jungle Book" *featuring the story of Mowgli, a boy raised by wolves. However, no case has ever been scientifically authenticated.*

petitor in hunting blackbuck and chinkara, but the cheetah is now extinct in India. The population of its normal food, however, has decreased considerably and so the wolf has been forced to move closer to rural areas, preying on sheep and goats. Sometimes in rare cases, some individual animals have carried off and eaten children, which naturally causes widespread terror. Dr. Jhala and Dinesh Kumar of the Wildlife Institute of India have studied many cases of "child-lifting" and felt that generally the "child-lifter" was a single animal. Nevertheless, all the wolves in the region naturally become suspect and every means, such as shooting, poisoning or trapping, is employed to destroy them. In the Hazaribagh Gazetteer published in 1910, the then Government offered a princely sum of Rs. 50 to anyone killing a man-eating wolf, which was twice the amount offered for a man-eating tiger! There are centuries-old stories in the villages of "wolf-children", where human children are brought up by a wolf pack. Such a belief was reflected in Rudyard Kipling's *Jungle Book* featuring the story of Mowgli, a boy raised by wolves. However, no case has ever been scientifically authenticated.

It has been estimated that the present wolf population is around 1500 in peninsular India. This number, however, is decreasing rapidly due to the destruction of its habitat, expanding human population and depleting prey species. It has had full protection since 1991 under the Wildlife Protection Act. Nevertheless, hunting and poisoning by the villagers continues in defence of their livestock.

Striped Hyena, *Hyaena hyaena:* There are four living species of the family Hyaenidae: the spotted hyena, the brown hyena, the aardwolf and the striped hyena, and the last is found in India. The hyena has a very important role in the food chain as it helps to keep the environment clean of dead animals. It generally feeds on the coarse remains and the tough bones of a dead animal, which are left by other forest scavengers like the vulture and jackal. It is also a predator in its own right. Due to its nocturnal habits and ungainly appearance, there is a lot of undeserved negative feeling against it, which needs to be corrected. Though it makes a living from carrion, it can also be a ferocious killer, especially when working in a pack like the spotted hyena. In some parts of Africa, such as Ngorongoro Crater in Tanzania, it is the most important of all the predators.

Right: *The hyena occasionally preys on sheep, goats, calves and stray dogs. It kills prey by holding it in its powerful jaws and violently shaking it till it dies.*

The striped hyena is a medium sized omnivore with a dog-like build and massive head. The slender front legs are longer than the back legs, which give it a very noticeable sloping back, from the well-developed forequarters to the less-developed hindquarters. The claws are short, blunt and non-retractable like a dog, and it walks on its toes. The coat colour varies from pale-grey to yellowish-buff and usually carries well-defined transverse stripes, which give it its common name. The height of the striped hyena is about 90 cm (3 feet), and weight about 34.5 to 38.5 kg (75 to 85 lb). The total length of the male is about 1.5 metres (5 feet). The female weighs about 4.5 kg (10 lb) less. The adult has a heavy dorsal crest of long erectile predominantly black hairs, from the base of the head to the root of the tail. On the central throat there is a prominent patch that extends upwards and outwards on both sides of the neck. The tail is short and bushy.

The striped hyena is found in India, South-western Asia and Northern Africa. In India, it is spread over a wide range extending right through the country. It is, however, not found in Assam and other adjoining states. Its preferred habitat is

Below: *The striped hyena has a very important role in the food chain as it helps to keep the environment free from dead animals. It generally feeds on the coarse remains and the tough bones of a dead animal, which are left by other forest scavengers like the vulture and jackal.*

grass and open jungles, the outskirts of a forest adjoining the plain, foothills, ravines and caves. Its vocalisation is one of the weirdest ever heard in the wilderness: an unearthly laughing chatter which is well known.

It generally lives in pairs, though sometimes a pack of five or six can be seen–probably members of a family group. It has a very acute power of scenting, which leads it to the carrion; its senses of eyesight and hearing are quite moderate. It is nocturnal in habit and retires before sunrise. It can crush strong bones in its powerful jaws and teeth and small pieces of undigested bones are often found in its chalky, calcium-rich feces. The hyena occasionally predates on sheep, goats, calves and stray dogs. It kills by holding its prey in its powerful jaws and violently shaking it till it dies. Its wide-ranging diet–and it eats anything edible–includes insects, reptiles, and fruits such as melons. It drinks regularly but can do without water for long periods, and live under desert conditions. Unfamiliar hyenas are aggressive when they meet and show it in a visual display by erection of the mane. The hyena generally lives within a home range but is not known to defend it. It generally moves at a speed of 2 to 4 km (1.24 to 2.5 miles) per hour or up to 8 km (5 miles) per hour when trotting. Dunbar Brander writes that the hyena will often annex the kills of the leopard. They prevent the return of the leopard and drive them off.

The striped hyena has not been studied much in the wild. There seems to be no particular breeding season but three to four blind cubs are born in a litter after a gestation period of 90 to 100 days. The nursery is some secluded cave or burrow. The pups have a silky white coat but no mane–this develops when they are adult. They open their eyes after 5 to 9 days. The mother brings solid food for the cubs to the den after about a month, and continues to nurse them until they are 4 to 5 months old. The average life span of a captive hyena is about 16 years.

Jackal, *Canis aureus indicus:* The Jackal enjoys a very low esteem in public view. Not many naturalists have thought it a worthy subject for study. One of the very few was C. H. Donald, who wrote in the *Bombay Natural History Journal,* Vol 47:721-729, 1948: "I wonder how many of my readers will look at the title with a commiserating smile and decline to read further. Jackals, indeed, what can anyone have to say about such dirty, skulking scavengers that is not already well known to every resident of India, or worth reading." He had kept many jackals as pets and found that not only were they very plucky but also very intelligent. He records "The natural intelligence, not necessarily the cunning engendered by centuries of life preservation, but the intelligence which denotes a high grade of thinking, is greater in a jackal than a dog." This is saying a lot, as the intelligence of a dog is well-known.

Left: *Jackal feeding on a chital kill in Kanha. Once the big cats leave a kill, first to arrive is the hyena followed by the jackal.*

The jackal is a very useful scavenger, complementary to the hyena in cleaning up the environment. Once the big cats leave a kill, first to arrive in the night is the hyena, followed by the jackal. As the dawn breaks, crows and vultures take up the scavenging. Where there is no human disturbance, the jackal comes to the carrion even during the day, while the vultures wait nearby to take their turn.

The jackal is found from North Africa, through the whole of Southern Europe and Asia up to Thailand. At one time it used to be well distributed throughout India but, mainly due to the extensive habitat destruction, it now occurs only in pockets. It inhabits grassy and open woodlands, humid forest tracts and scrub environment. It is at home in Himalayas up to an altitude of 3660 metres (12000 feet) and lives near many hill stations around the country. It is comfortable living in the vicinity of human habitations, sheltering in dense grass, burrows or among ruins around small towns and villages. Its long-drawn, wailing cry repeated three or four times at dusk, then taken up by others of the species, must be familiar to many people in India. Its calls leading to a crescendo then fading out, sometimes reminded me of the calls of the Brainfever birds at the foothills of the Himalayas! Its coat has a uniform colour between dirty yellow and reddish brown and the reddish tail has a black finish. There is considerable variation in the colouration and size; bluish-slate coloured animals are more frequent in the forests. It is somewhat similar to a wolf, though smaller in build; the wolf looks much bolder. The height of the jackal is 38 to 43 cm (15 to 17 inches); its length from head to root of tail 60 to 75 cm (24 in to 30 inches); the

“The jackals long-drawn, wailing cry repeated three or four times at dusk, then taken up by others of the species, must be familiar to many people in India.”

Overleaf: *Indian fox sitting.*

tail is 20 to 27 cm (8 to 11 inches) and its weight is between 8 to 11 kg (17 to 25 lb). The animals from north India are on an average bigger and heavier in build than those found in the south.

In addition to scavenging on tiger and leopard kills, the jackal also predates on small living creatures such as the young of deer and antelopes, rodents, jungle birds, insects and poultry. It also eats fruits like melon and ber. It is monogamous and conjugally faithful and normally lives in a pair, but has been known to hunt in packs. The pair lives together, hunts together and raises a family together. Once I saw a pair hunt down a chital doe and then take turns in feeding; one patiently sitting nearby keeping watch while the other fed.

The jackal is hunted by man for its fur and in the South villagers organise special hunts on some religious festivals. Efforts are being made by many NGOs to persuade them to give up this cruel practice. The leopard is its main predator in the forest.

Indian Fox, *Vulpes bengalensis:* From time immemorial, the fox has found a place in the folklores and mythologies of many countries, especially European. Perhaps its nocturnal habits, long pointed face, devious way of running with its tail held horizontally, and solitary and cunning nature have cast it in an unfavourable light. Over 2500 years ago, Aesop wove many classic stories around it, conveying some moral points. One such most quoted story is of 'The Fox and the Grapes', which conveys the fact that people often give face-saving excuses for their failures

The fox is a medium-sized carnivore belonging to the dog family. There are fourteen species, of which the red fox and the Indian fox are found in India. The red fox lives in the Himalayas from Kashmir, Ladakh up to Sikkim, and its range extends North as far as the shores of Arctic lands. The Indian fox is patchily distributed across the whole of India from the Himalayan foothills to Kanyakumari in the south. It is a beautiful, sleek animal, smaller and slimmer than the red fox. It has a sandy-orange to grayish coat with a black-tipped tail, whitish belly and, sometimes, orangish legs. Its head-to-body length is 45 to 60 cm (18 to 24 inches); its tail 25 to 35 cm (10 to 14 inches) and its standing height is less than 30 cm (1 foot). It weighs about 1.8 to 3.2 kg (4 to 7 lb). This fox is indigenous to India, and lives in grasslands, scrubs in flat and rocky areas avoiding forests, and is common near cultivation bordering irrigation canals. Its life span is about 14 years.

It lives in a self-dug burrow, or adapted porcupine bur-

Below: *An Indian fox standing. It is a beautiful, sleek animal, smaller and slimmer than the red fox.*

row, in the ground or an embankment, with many escape openings and central chamber, 60 to 90 cm (2 to 3 feet) under ground. It is crepuscular in habit, but in grasslands with less human disturbance it can be seen in the morning also, especially on cloudy days. Like the jackal, it is believed to live in a long-term monogamous pairing. It is a solitary hunter, using its eyes, ears and nose to detect its prey. It then carefully stalks and pounces upon it when close enough. The prey is killed by holding it in the mouth and violently shaking it. Extra food is sometimes cached in a hole dug with the feet, the earth swept back with the snout being similar to a dog hiding a bone. The Indian fox preys on small mammals, reptiles, poultry and ground-nesting jungle birds. At the outset of monsoon, winged termites are also much relished as they emerge from their mounds. It also eats fruits such as melon, ber and the pods of *Cicer arietum*. Though not much

Left: *It is the long legged build of the jungle cat that is immortalised in the Egyptian statues of cats which honour the Goddess Bast! In artwork, it was depicted hunting with humans and their mummified remains are common in tombs of the period.*

appreciated, it does a great service to farmers by feeding on crop-damaging rodents, grasshoppers and other insects. It has a variety of vocalization, from yelping to a chattering cry. Its main defence against enemies is its fast get-away speed, and the devious twists and turns it takes while running. It can sustain a speed of about 30 kph (18 mph) over long distance.

The Indian fox generally breeds during the cold season and bears 3 to 4 cubs at a time, between February and April after a gestation period of 51 to 53 days. The cubs weigh about 50 to 65g (1.5 to 2.5 oz) each at birth and are born blind and helpless in the central chamber of the burrow. Both the parents take care of the young and for the first few weeks feed them on regurgitated meat. The cubs come out after about 5 weeks and spend a lot of their time playing outside in the morning and evening. At the slightest disturbance they immediately disappear into the burrow. When they are about 5 months old, they start some hunting on their own.

Though the fox is a farmer's friend that keeps a check on agricultural pests, it is hunted for its pelt, and for its flesh and bones out of superstitious belief. In Karnataka, some communities organise hunts to capture it for sacrificial purposes during some religious festivals. Efforts are being made to educate the villagers to desist from such cruel practices.

Jungle Cat, *Felis chaus:* The jungle cat is widely found in the northern parts of Africa to southeastern Asia. Its extensive range has resulted in noticeable differences, including variations in colour and size. It is found in India from the Himalayas to the southern tip. It may be seen in the interior of dense forests, or in a grass patch in the open plains or in marshy, wet environments. It is a medium-sized animal considerably larger than the domestic cat, but smaller than a jackal. It has long legs but a short tail, and the eyes are pale green. It is typically of sandy-brown colour, with no distinctive body markings but there are sometimes, transverse stripes on the upper parts of the legs and a ringed tail with black tip. Its tracks are similar to the pugmarks of the tiger and leopard, but on a much smaller scale. Its head-to-body length is 56 to 94 cm (22 to 39 inches), and the tail is 20 to 30 cm (8 to 12 inches) long. The male weighs about 6 kg (13 lb) and the female of the species about 4 kg (8.4 lb).

The jungle cat is diurnal in habits, and is seen mostly in the morning and evening although it also hunts at night. It preys on rabbits, small mammals, birds, frogs, reptiles and insects. It sometimes brings down the young of small ungulates, especially of the spotted deer (chital). It has very acute hearing, which helps it to locate the prey even in dense vegetation. It is known to jump as high as two metres (6 feet) to catch flying birds. It is a bold animal and Prater mentions a case of its entering a village and seizing poultry even in the presence of their owners. As it was destructive to game birds, in the old 'shikar' days it was recommended that it should be destroyed whenever possible!

It is not easily seen these days in India, the main reason being habitat shrinkage. It is also being killed by man for its habit of raiding poultry and for its soft pelt, although hunting it is legally prohibited in India.

There are two breeding seasons: in January and April and then again in August and November. After a gestation period of 53 to 56 days, 3 to 4 kittens are born in a reed nest, abandoned burrow or some other secluded place. The young are quite different in colour from the adults, generally greyer and having black tabby markings on their coats. The young are weaned by 8 weeks and are on their own after about 3 months. Sexual maturity is reached by the age of 18 months.

It is the long-legged build of the jungle cat that is immortalised in the Egyptian statues of cats that honour the Goddess Bast! In artwork, it was depicted hunting with humans and their mummified remains are common in tombs of the period.

Marsh Crocodile, *Crocodylus palustris:* Crocodilians, similar to the present day crocodiles, appeared on the earth about 190 million years ago. The word, crocodylus is derived from the Greek 'krokodeilos', which means 'pebble worm', referring to the general appearance of a crocodile. The word 'palustris' means 'marshy' or 'swampy', which is the habitat where it lives. Hence, it has been given the common name 'Marsh Crocodile'.

It is primarily found on the Indian subcontinent, Bangladesh and extending into Pakistan and Sri Lanka. Its elongated body with long muscular paddle tail is well adapt-

Below: *Marsh crocodile basking over rock.*

ed to its amphibian way of life. Its important sense organs, the eyes and ear openings and the external nostril openings, are on the upper side of its head, which normally remains above the water surface when the rest of the body is submerged. Membranous flaps close its nostrils when the animal fully submerges under water. A similar flap in front of the interior nostril openings creates a rear closure to the mouth cavity, permitting the crocodile to breathe even if under water. Similarly its ears are protected from water by movable external membranous flaps. Each eye has a thin translucent membrane, permitting limited underwater vision. The colour of the juvenile is light tan with black cross banding on body and tail. The adult is olive above with little banding remaining.

Above: *Sambar passing a marsh crocodile in Ranthambhore.*

The crocodiles are the largest and heaviest of all the reptiles. Their average length is about 2 to 3 metres (6 to 9 feet), which can go up to 4 to 5 metres (13 to 16 feet). The size is age related and the female crocodile matures at a younger age than the male. Like all nocturnal animals, it has vertical slit-shaped pupils, which narrow in bright light and widen in darkness thus permitting it to see even in very low light. The jaws are jagged and carry rows of sharp teeth, which are replaced regularly by new ones growing from below. It cannot bring out its thick, fleshy tongue since it is firmly attached to the floor of the mouth. The rear of the head forms a flat plate to which the short, powerful neck is attached. The upper surface of the back and the tail is covered with large horny plates. The legs are short, but powerful enough to support its weight when walking or running on the ground. The forefeet have five toes and the hind legs have only four toes, which are wholly or partially webbed. It spends most of its time floating and swimming in water, but from time to time, it emerges to bask in the sun on the bank or over a rock. The crocodile sometimes basks with wide-open mouth, which is a method of heat control. It is a silent reptile, but hisses loudly and thrashes its tail about, when it feels threatened. Another vocalisation is a roar resembling the bellow of cattle. There is little information available about its longevity. A crocodile in captivity seldom lives beyond about 40 years, probably due to lack of exercise and little variety in diet.

The crocodile is well adapted to an amphibian life and lives not only in natural lakes, ponds and marshes but also in man-made large reservoirs and irrigation ponds. It prefers shallow water not deeper than 5 metres (15 feet) and avoids fast moving rivers. It is carnivorous, feeding on fish, frogs, and crustaceans, and birds and mammals, that come to the water's edge to drink. To catch land mammals it lies at the edge of the water or submerged near it, waiting for a potential victim. It either knocks its prey into the water with a blow of the tail or grabs the legs in its jaws and drowns it in the water. "The recorded stomach contents of a crocodile include leopard, wild dog, hyena, chital, sambar, nilgai fawn, four-horned antelope, barking deer, monkeys, domestic dog, goats, calves, pig, ducks and a variety of wild birds." (J.C.Daniel).

"The recorded stomach contents of a crocodile include leopard, wild dog, hyena, chital, sambar, nilgai fawn, four-horned antelope, barking deer, monkeys, domestic dog, goats, calves, pig, ducks and a variety of wild birds."

Its breeding season is from mid-January in the south, to March in the northern parts of the country. It has a hierarchal social system, with the most powerful animal becoming the dominant animal, and establishes a territory prior to courtship and mating. Mating is usually in water or on the rocks pock-marking the rivers. The female lays from 10 to 48 or more hard-shelled eggs in a clutch, after a gestation period of 55 to 75 days. In captivity, it has been known to lay two clutches in one year but reliable data in the wild is not known. The eggs are deposited by the female into a burrow dug by her in the ground. It is dug more or less horizontally, just above the water line, and may be several metres long ending in a nest chamber. After two or three months of incubation, the young are fully developed and ready to hatch. They then make ultrasonic squeaking noises, which are recognised by the mother. She digs up the nest, transports the hatchlings in her mouth to a nursery pool, and keeps watch over them for about two months as they grow. Baby crocodiles feed on small fish, insects and small invertebrates. For the first four years or so, the young grow at the rate of about 30 cm (1 foot) per year, and then growth decreases. The young remain in loose association with the parents for about one year before dispersing.

“Suddenly one goose, cackling loudly, was powerfully pulled underneath as it tried to take-off with wings violently flapping.”

The species was previously threatened by illegal hunting for skins, which were much in demand as leather for shoes, handbags and other luxuries. The main threat now is from habitat alteration and destruction such as dam projects, mortality in fishing nets, egg collection and the use of parts for medicinal purposes. Its status has been declared as vulnerable in the IUCN Red List; the current management is based principally on legal protection and large-scale breeding and rearing programmes.

Indian Python, *python molurus:* Out of 16 species of pythons in the world, two are found in India. One is the Indian python or rock python, which is found throughout India and also in Pakistan and Sri Lanka. Its maximum length is about 6 metres (18 feet), the average being 4 to 5 metres (12 to 15 feet). The longest python found was from Cooch Behar in West Bengal and measured 5.85 metres (19 feet 2 inches). Its maximum recorded weight was 90.7 kg (200 lb), though the average is much less. Its habitat is dense as well as open forests, scrub land and rocky hillsides. It prefers tracts near areas of water. The other species, the reticulated python, grows much longer and a female specimen was measured at 8.4 metres (28 feet) long and weighed 113.6 kg (250 lb). The reticulated python occurs in India only in the areas bordering Myanmar and in Nicobar Islands.

The eyes of the python are small and the pupil is vertical. The short prehensile tails tapers rapidly and has a spur on each side of the anus, which can inflict serious injury. These spurs are vestigial legs remnants of the days of its lizard-like ancestors. The skin is a yellowish-grey colour, with a series of dark brown, irregular patches from the neck to tail. The intricate ground-coloured patterns on its body enables the python to blend in its natural habitat. The lower lip is often mottled and the head carries a dark-brown lance-shaped mark with a blackish outline. The Indian python is a heavily built snake and is ordinarily sluggish in its movements. I have, however, seen it move very fast. Once I was looking for them near the Python Point at Bharatpur Bird Sanctuary the famous wintering ground of the highly endangered Siberian cranes. Arati disturbed a python resting under a bush and it moved so fast that only a mere blur was recorded on a high-speed film. We once saw a python swimming in a water body at Bharatpur with just the tip of the mouth showing above the surface. It submerged about 10 metres (30 feet) away from a flock of bar-headed geese. Suddenly one goose, cackling loudly, was powerfully pulled underneath as it tried to take off with wings violently flapping. The very fact that it can immobilise a fast animal like a deer speaks of the swiftness with which it strikes its prey. The python has been known to catch even porcupines, which stick out their quills almost instantaneously at the slightest alarm. Although large pythons mostly remain on the ground, they can easily climb trees and sometimes ambush their prey from overhead branches overlooking paths frequented by jungle animals.

The python mainly preys on warm-blooded animals such as rodents, birds and small and large forest mammals. It also preys on other reptiles. It prefers large mammals, since a big meal satisfies its hunger for a long period, sometimes for many months. It shows great alacrity once it locates its victim, it hurls itself at the prey and rapidly wraps its powerful coils round and round exerting tremendous pressure, suffocating it to death. It then uncoils and rests for some time, before examining the prey with the tongue, which is an organ of smell, and beginning to swallow–always head first. The head is held in its backward curving teeth and the prey is forced in by rhythmic jaw and muscle movements. It is a reversible process so the python can regurgitate its prey if it is disturbed or in case the large prey inside comes in the way of quick get away. The jaw structure is loosely articulated and the two halves are joined only by elastic ligaments. The swallowing capacity is thus limited only by the elasticity of the skin. This allows the python to extend the jaws even up to an angle of 180°. The python ignores man; in fact, like all wildlife it shuns human beings. It is, however, known to have a vicious bite that can turn septic unless treated immediately. A large reptile can swallow a prey up to 70 kg (155 lb) in weight. In north

India, the python hibernates during winter in any convenient place such as a tree-hole, in a burrow or under rocks.

The Indian python becomes sexually mature at about 5 years of age, when about 3.35 metres (11 feet) in length. The male stimulates the female by stroking her with his anal spurs. He then wraps around the female and they mate. After three to four months, the female lays her eggs in a tree hole or rock crevices, with from 8 to 100 eggs in a clutch, each measuring about 12 x 6 cm (4.7 x 2.4 inches). The eggs are leathery, white in colour and domed at both ends. The mother coils around the clutch throughout the almost 58-day incubation period, leaving the nest only to drink. The eggs are kept warm by controlling her body temperature, shivering when the air temperature makes it necessary. The mother, however, takes no further interest in her brood after hatching. The young have many natural enemies like the eagle, crocodile,

Above: *A python near its den. It shows great alacrity once it locates its victim. It hurls itself at the prey and rapidly wraps its powerful coils round and round exerting tremendous pressure, suffocating it to death.*

tiger, leopard and hyena. The lifespan of the python is said to be between 20 to 30 years: the recorded life in captivity is 22 years.

The Indian python is endangered throughout its range. The main threat is from habitat destruction and hunting for the skin-trade–its skin is widely sought for making shoes, belts and other luxury items. Its usual habitat is also disappearing to make way for human settlement and cultivation. The python is listed in CITES Appendix 1 and all trade in live python or its skin is prohibited. Poaching, however, remains a threat and illegal trade continues; some tribes in India kill it for its meat.

Hindu mythology mentions King Nala finding his wife Damayanti entwined by a python as he returned from an errand in a jungle. There are many stories of pythons swallowing man but only a few are accepted by zoologists. A few instances are mentioned in *Men and Snakes* by Ramona and Desmond Morris. The case of a drunk, who fell asleep in a gutter, is one of them. A python swallowed his left leg till the gaping jaws reached his trunk. His screams brought succour, but it was too late. The snake had been digesting the leg and only an immediate amputation at the hospital saved his life. There was another reported case of a 14-year-old boy, who was swallowed by a 5.5 metre (18 feet) python in the East Indies. There was a press report on 1 December 1986, of Nanaiah, a middle aged man who was attacked by a 6 metre (20 feet) python as he was walking through the Markhut forest in Coorg district of Karnataka. His desperate cries attracted forest officials who "found to their horror that one third of Nanaiah's body had already been swallowed by the reptile." He was rescued and hospitalised. These must be exceptional cases as the python generally does not attack man and in fact is sometimes kept as a pet.

Ruddy Mongoose, *Herpestes smithi:* The mongoose is perhaps best known for its ability to kill poisonous snakes, especially cobras. At one time, it used to be exhibited by itinerant snake charmers, who showed both a mongoose and a cobra but naturally did not allow them to fight. Its prowess is celebrated by Rudyard Kipling in his book, *Jungle Book,* in which a mongoose, Rikki Tikki-Tavi, fights and kills a pair of cobras. The original home of the mongoose is believed to be Africa and from there, one of the genus, Herpestes, has spread to Spain and southern Asia. Six species of this genus are found in Asia and all are represented in India.

The mongoose is a small, short-legged animal, long-bodied with a pointed nose, small semi-circular ears and a long furry tail. The fur is brownish freckled with lighter grey. The main difference between a common mongoose and ruddy mongoose is that the tail of the common mongoose is tipped white or yellowish-red, while that of the ruddy species is tipped black. It is nearly 90 cm (3 feet) in length, including

Below: *The ruddy mongoose preys upon rodent, reptile, scorpion and other smaller animals, as well as insects. It sometimes subdues larger creatures by the speed and ferocity of a headlong attack.*

the tail, which is about 45 cm (18 inches) long. There are five digits on each foot and the fore claws are sharp and curved, designed for digging. The ear is made up of complicated folds, which can completely protect the ear opening from dust when digging. The common mongoose, *H. edwardsi,* and the small Indian mongoose, *H. auropunctatus,* are found throughout India from the Himalayan foothills to Kanyakumari. The ruddy mongoose, however, is a denizen of the forests of central and southern India.

The mongoose is a very bold and agile predatory animal. It has an important role in the forest, not only as a camp follower of the tiger, but also as a biological controller of birds and smaller animals. When in danger, it erects its long hair and fights back fiercely. It preys upon rodent, reptile, scorpion and other smaller animals as well as insects. It sometimes subdues larger creatures by the speed and ferocity of a headlong attack. It also raids nests and eats both eggs and the chicks of birds. The ruddy mongoose is especially fond of large snails and also feeds on carrion and on fruits and other vegetable matters. On locating a prey too far away for pouncing, it will stalk until it gets up close, or follow the quarry to its burrow and dig it out. The powers of sight, hearing and scenting are well developed in the mongoose. It lives in a burrow, hollow of a log or tree, rock crevice or in bushes. It kills snakes like cobra by its extraordinary agility in avoiding a strike and then catching it once the snake is tired, by the back of the head and biting it through. Sometimes the fight can continue for an hour or more. It is believed that the mongoose has a better immunity from snake poison than most other animals. It breeds all the year round and up to three litters may be produced in a year. The period of gestation is about 60 days. The ruddy mongoose is similar to the common mongoose in habits, food and breeding.

Vulture, *Accipiitridae:* Rather ungainly and much maligned, the vulture is perhaps the most reliable and efficient camp follower of the tiger. At times, we have located a tiger kill, or a tiger resting near a kill, by just observing the movement of vultures in the jungle. If vultures are gliding into a particular area, there is likely to be a few-hours-old kill lying there. If they are sitting on a tree, along with crows and tree pies, looking down, most probably the predator is still on the kill. Given the opportunity, around 30 vultures can finish off a large sambar stag kill within half an hour. The primary responsibility for keeping the environment clean has been assigned by Nature to a variety of carrion eaters, the vulture possibly being its most ubiquitous and efficient agent.

"At times, we have located a tiger kill, or a tiger resting near a kill, by just observing the movement of vultures in the jungle."

Eight species of vulture are found in India, including the very large Bearded vulture (Lammergeier), which is found in the Himalayas and associated northern mountains. Generally in peninsular India, the Whitebacked Vulture *Gyps bengalensis,* Longbilled Vulture *Gyps indicus,* and King Vulture *Sarcogyps calvus,* are seen–the first two being traditionally more common. They are of the size of a peacock but without the tail. Their powerful hooked beak and naked head are designed for tearing and eating animal carcass. The Whitebacked Vulture is a heavy, dark-brown bird with a thin and bony head and neck, and a white back conspicuous in flight. The Longbilled Vulture *Gyps indicus,* is similar but without the white back. The Black or King Vulture, which is not very numerous, has a deep blood-red head and neck, with white down on the breast, large black beak and prominently hanging red wattles. It is higher in the vulture hierarchy because of its body size and more powerful beak and claws. Other vultures make way for the King Vulture once it lands near the kill and take their turn after it to feed. All vultures, however, give way to the mammalian scavengers, the hyena and jackal. The much smaller White Scavenger or Egyptian Vulture *Nephron percnopterus,* also is sometimes seen at carrion, but gets the last chance to feed.

The vultures nest 10 to 15 metres (30 to 45 feet) high in tall trees such as *ficus spp. Azadaritica indica, Dalberga sisso,* in which they make a large untidy nest of sticks or twigs and lay a single white egg. The nesting season is December to April for the King Vulture and October to March for the other two species.

The vultures also carry out their role of environment cleaning in the towns and villages. A number of these birds will be found feeding on garbage dumps near towns. In India, after the removal of the hide from dead cattle, the carcasses are kept outside the villages for the vultures, which strip it to mere bones within 20 to 30 minutes. The vulture is built for long hours in the air on its broad wings. Like an unpowered glider, it makes use of thermals to soar high in the sky patrolling for information about any dead animal. It has an extremely sharp vision and can either see the carcass of a dead animal, or the movements of other scavengers like crow, from a long distance. It has an unusually long, naked neck enabling it to reach deep inside the carcass to feed.

The population of Indian vultures, especially the Gyps genus, has been declining at an alarming rate during the last decade. Dr.Vibhu Prakash of the Bombay Natural History Society (BNHS) was the first to notice this decline at the Keoladev Ghana Bird Sanctuary. The major cause of this massive decline was the high mortality rate and breeding failure of the Gyps species. There used to be a colony of a few thousand Whitebacked and Longbilled Vultures at Bayana near

Bharatpur a few years ago; it has now come down to a mere 50 or 60 vultures. They suffered from a mysterious disease, which began in the early 1990s and has multiplied to epidemic proportions. A sign of the deadly disease seems to be the head drooping for long periods, with the eyes closed and feathers ruffled. This continues for nearly a month and then the bird simply drops dead. The Poultry Diagnostic Research Centre (PDRC) of Pune, along with BNHS, is carrying out research to identify the reason, but the cause is still not fully known. Unless some solution to control the problem is found soon, there could be unimaginable consequences on the environmental health of the country, since it still depends on vultures for carcass disposal.

Right: *Vultures approaching a chital kill. The vulture is built for long hours in the air on its broad wings. Like an unpowered glider, it makes use of thermals to soar high in the sky patrolling for information about any dead animal. It has an extremely sharp vision and can either see the carcass of a dead animal, or the movements of other scavengers like crow, from a long distance.*

“The aggressor had had the best of it, for the party found the remains of the elephant calf and the dead tusker's huge bulk, atrociously torn, but the tiger had disappeared.”

THE PREY SPECIES

THE EARLIEST MAMMALS, like their reptilian ancestors, were active predators. During their evolutionary phase, the species developed separately according to their food adaptation. The stronger and more ferocious species, which could feed on other species, became carnivores and occupied the top of the food pyramid. They became the secondary or tertiary consumers of herbivores, the primary consumers. The herbivores lived on green plants, which produced their own food from inorganic materials utilising the sun's energy and became producers. There was thus a natural path of food consumption, called a food chain, showing who ate whom and the flow of energy and nutrients from producers to the primary and secondary consumers. The green plants are the

Left: *A real wildlife photographer? The camera was set up for photographing a shy family of spotted owlet near their nest-hole in a tree at Bharatpur Bird Sanctuary. A curious chital comes out of the elephant grass to investigate.*

producers; herbivores are the primary consumers and the carnivores, like tiger, the secondary consumers.

Prey Species

The tiger can live on a diversity of prey species. Its preference, however, is for larger prey, such as deer, wild boar, gaur, young elephant and rhino, up to about 450 kg (1000 lb), which can take care of its hunger for a few days. But it also feeds on monkeys, peacock, or even fish or frogs when driven by hunger. Porcupine is another favourite prey, though the tiger is sometimes injured by its quills which could become a cause of it becoming a man-eater as it becomes difficult for it to catch its normal prey.

The deer are perhaps the earliest of all the ruminants, first appearing in the lower Miocene period. Its size then was very small and it did not have antlers. Later antlers developed; they

Below: *Chital deer running. The tiger is their main predator, though they have to be ever alert against leopard and wild dog also. Hyena and jackals also prey upon fawns. Chital have good sight but their powers of scenting and hearing are even more acute.*

are just solid bones that are shed and regrown every year. During the rutting season, the antlers are of maximum size with a solid bone structure stripped of the soft skin covering called velvet. Afterwards they fall off, grow again and are in best shape before the next rutting season. The antlers are needed not only for defence against predators, but also to fight off competitors during rutting season. The social system of the deer is largely matriarchal–except during the brief rutting season, the mature stags live in loose bachelor groups.

There are eight species of deer found in India: sambar *Cervus unicolor;* chital *Axis axis;* barasingha *Cervus duvauceli;* hangul or Kashmir stag *Cervus elaphus hanglu;* Thamin or Manipur deer *Cervus eldi;* hog deer *Axis porcinus;* barking deer *Muntiacus muntjak* and Musk deer *Moschus moschiferus*. The sambar, which lives in dense forest, is territorial but the chital moves from herd to herd in search of mate. Sambar, chital and barking deer are found in most of the forests throughout India, Sri Lanka and Nepal. Barasingha is now found only in Assam, the kheri region of Uttar Pradesh and in Kanha, Madhya Pradesh. The hangul inhabits the north side of the Kashmir valley and some of the adjacent valleys. The thamin is highly endangered and is found only in the Keibul Lamjao Sanctuary in the state of Manipur. The smaller deer, hog deer, barking deer and musk deer, are of solitary nature and it is rare to find two or three together. The hog deer is found in the grassy plains of northern India and Sri Lanka; the barking deer or muntjak inhabits thickly forested areas of India; and musk deer live in the Himalayas from central India to north-eastern Asia.

Chital or Spotted Deer, *Axis axis:* The chital is, perhaps, the most beautiful and graceful deer in the world. It is a medium sized deer with large soulful eyes and is ubiquitous in India and Sri Lanka, wherever there is jungle with good grazing and availability of water. It feeds on tender grass shoots in the meadows along forest edges, and also seeks leaves and fruits. It grazes in the open until late in the morning up to 10:30am, and again after about 3:30pm in the evening. It stands about 91 cm (36 inches) at the withers. Its glossy coat is bright red-dish brown with white spots and is whitish below. The coat looks its best in the winter and rainy season. A dark stripe trails down the back from neck to the end of the tail.

Only the stags grow antlers, which can be up to 100 cm (40 inches) long. The antlers have three tines, a long brow line curving almost at right angles to the beam and two branch tines at the top. Most of the chital shed their antlers by August and soon start growing them again. At first, the antlers are covered in velvet, which they rub off against bushes or trees. The antlers are in full glory by March and the stags are ready to fight other stags for hinds. The fight can be fierce and can lead even to the death of one of the contestants. Generally, the defeated stag chooses to run away and is then seldom chased by the winner. There is no well-defined rutting season and some stags with hard antlers are seen, and their harsh bellowing heard, almost throughout the year. Schaller in his book, *The Deer And The Tiger,* has, however, recorded that most fawns are born between January and May in Kanha.

“The alarm call of the chital is a staccato “Ku”,“Ku”,“Ku”, sometimes accompanied by stamping on the ground.”

The chital are prolific breeders and young are dropped every six months or so. Generally, only one fawn is born though Dunbar Brander has recorded in his book, *Wild Animals In Central India,* that one to three fawns are born at a time, two being a common number. In my experience, I have only once seen a hind with two fawns at Ranthambhore. She was suckling one and affectionately licking the other.

The tiger is their main predator, though they have to be ever alert against leopard and wild dog also. Hyena and jackals also prey upon fawns. Chital have good sight, but their powers of scenting and hearing are even more acute. They can always sense any unusual movement, but if one freezes when they look up from their activity, they do not become alarmed and resume their activity after some time. On 30 March, 2001, Arati and I were travelling in a jeep on the Salghat Road of the Kanha National Park. We saw a tigress at about 5 pm near Bhapsa Behra with some small prey in her mouth. She went into an area of small dense cover and could not be seen. At about 5:25 pm, a herd of about 20 chital approached the patch where the tigress was hiding. The herd suddenly stopped about 100 yards away and their leader carefully approached the cover with raised tail. She sniffed the air a few times and gave the alarm call. The herd immediately ran away. We did not think that she could have seen the tigress, but the wind direction was favourable so she could scent the big cat from about 75 yards and confirm the suspicion of the herd.

The alarm call of the chital is a staccato "Ku", "Ku", "Ku", sometimes accompanied by stamping on the ground. The call of a single chital does not necessarily signify the presence of a predator. A doe sometimes calls if she misses her young. Once I hastened to a patch where a stag was repeatedly calling, only to find that it was courting a hind! However, if a number of deer give the alarm call, the presence of a predator is always indicated. The chital and common langurs have a unique symbiotic relationship. Chital keep observation from the ground whereas monkeys watch from a height. One is likely to find chital under a tree on which langurs are feeding. The langurs drop fruits and leaves from the tree, which are eagerly sought by the chital. On observing any suspicious movement, the monkeys go to the top of the tree and if a predator is located, they give their alarm call, which is taken up by the deer and the whole forest goes on alert. Inside the forest, the chital are quite tolerant of any moving vehicle. However, if the vehicle stops near them, they take alarm and run away. The same deer herd assembles near the tourist cottages in late evening and passes the night not far from human habitation. It is obvious that they sense more safety there than inside the forest, where the nocturnal predators roam in search of prey.

In the end, there cannot be a better and more poetic description of the chital than the one quoted by Champion from the writing of *Hawkeye,* in his book *With A Camera In Tiger-Land:* "Imagine a forest glade, the graceful bamboo arching overhead to form a lovely vista, with here and there bright spots and deep shadows-the effect of the sun's rays struggling to penetrate the leafy roof of Nature's aisle. Deep in the solitude of the woods see now the dappled herd, and watch the handsome buck as he roams here and there in the midst of his harem, or browsing among the bushes, exhibits his graceful antlers to the lurking foe, who, by patient woodcraft, has succeeded in approaching his unsuspecting victim; observe how proudly he holds himself as some other buck of less pretensions dares to approach the ladies of the group; see how he advances on tip-toe, all the hairs on his body standing on end, and with a thundering rush drives headlong away this bold intruder and then comes swaggering back! But hark, a twig has broken! Suddenly the buck wheels round, facing the quarter from whence the sound proceeded. Look at him now and say, is he not a quarry well worthy of a hunter's notice?"

Right: *Sambar stag standing to browse.*

"With head erect, antlers thrown back, his white throat exposed, his tail raised, his whole body gathered together prepared to bound away into the deep forest in the twinkling of an eye, he stands-a splendid specimen of the cervine tribe. We will not kill him; we look back and admire. Then a hind gives an imperceptible signal, and the next moment the whole herd has dashed through the bamboo alleys, vanishing from sight–a dappled hide now and again in the sunlight as its owner scampers away to more distant haunts."

Above: *The adult male sambar bears long three-tined antlers, with two brow tines and main beams forked into two tines near the top.*

Sambar, *Cervus unicolor:* The sambar is the largest deer found in India, Nepal and Southeast Asia. It is slightly bigger than even the Kashmir Stag *Cervus elaphus hangulu,* which is found in the Kashmir valley. The stags stand up to 122 to 212 cm (48 to 56 inches) at the shoulder and the length of the body is from 182 cm to 230 cm (6 to 7 feet) with the tail length of 30 to 33 cm (12 to 13 inches). There are several races of sambar, the largest is the Indian and the smallest is found in Malaysia. The average weight of the stag varies from 186 kg to 202 kg (410 to 445 lb). It is a hill loving animal and can be found at an altitude of up to 2135 to 2440 metres (7000 to 8000 feet). Rugged hilly slopes with dense and deep forest are its preferred habitat.

It comes out in the open to feed at dusk and retires to its hilly cover after dawn. It is a grazer as well as a browser and feeds chiefly on green and coarse grass along forest pools and nullahs, and browses on the tender shoots and fruits of a variety of plants. In season, it can be seen eating the white flowers of the mahua *Bassia latifolia* tree, which can ferment inside the stomach and make them slightly intoxicated. The fruits of the Amla *Phyllanthus emblica* tree are also a favourite food. It also eats the barks of certain trees such as Haldua *Adina cordifolia*. Sankhala records in his book, *Tiger*, that the sambar can browse up to a height of 2.7 metres (9 feet) when standing on its hind legs, can clear up to 3.4 metres (11 feet) to reach some particularly choice fruit, and will wade through up to 2.1 metres (7 feet). of water to feed on aquatic vegetation, especially lotus and water lilies and even trapha and algae.

The coats of does and fawns are generally reddish-brown in colour, while that of an old stag is almost dark with a ruff around the neck and throat. The winter coat is thicker and richer in shade. We have observed that in southern India, sambar sometimes develop a sore patch on the throat but its cause is not exactly known. The animal, however, does not appear to be in much discomfort and carries on with its normal activities. Dunbar Brander writes that sambar in Assam area are also afflicted by this curious phenomenon.

Similar to the chital stag, the male sambar bears long three-tined antlers, with two brow tines and main beams forked into two tines near the top. The full-grown antlers are massive, corrugated and dark brown in colour and whitish at the tips. At the base, the girth may be as much as 20 cm (8 inches). The antlers are shed at the onset of summer in March-beginning of April. They start regrowing within a month and velvet is cleared by November so they will be in their full glory in winter. The length of the horn from pedicle to tip on average is about 100 cm (40 inches); the record head according to Gordon Graham, came from the then Bhopal State and was 127.32cm (50·125 inches).

The sambar is a shy animal of solitary habits, but may associate with two or three stags for most of the year–except during the rutting season. This season varies from the Himalayas to the plains. According to Schaller, the rutting season extends from October to December in peninsular India while the spring is the mating season in the Himalayas. The male will then fight for its territory and its small harem. When in full rut, it will sometimes wallow in mud pools and carry dried mud cakes on its coat. It also occasionally thrashes grass, saplings and bushes and struts about with the tattered remains adorning its antlers, which are rock hard at this time. Each adult doe bears a young once a year, after a gestation period of eight months. It is rare for two fawns to be born at a time. After the breeding season, the sambar returns to its solitary existence.

The tiger is the chief predator and sambar is its preferred prey. It provides food to the tiger for many days and respite from the necessity of arduous hunting for some time. The main defence of the sambar is its swiftness. If it is not brought down by the tiger within its first onrush of 46 metres (50 yards) or so, the tiger gives up the chase. The sambar has a very acute sense of hearing and scenting–being a dweller of deep forests, it has to depend mainly on olfactory and auditory cues for survival. As an adaptive mechanism, its ears are larger than other deer and can detect even the slightest sound. Its abrupt alarm call, which sounds like "ponk," is a sign that it has heard or scented a suspicious presence. A repeat call accompanied by stamping of the ground is a sure indication of the presence of a tiger. Its short and sudden call, heard close by, can be quite unnerving. It often returns to investigate the source of its suspicion and this curiosity sometimes proves fatal.

Barasingha or Swamp Deer, *Cervus duvaucelii:* The name Barasingha literally means a deer which carries twelve (*barah*

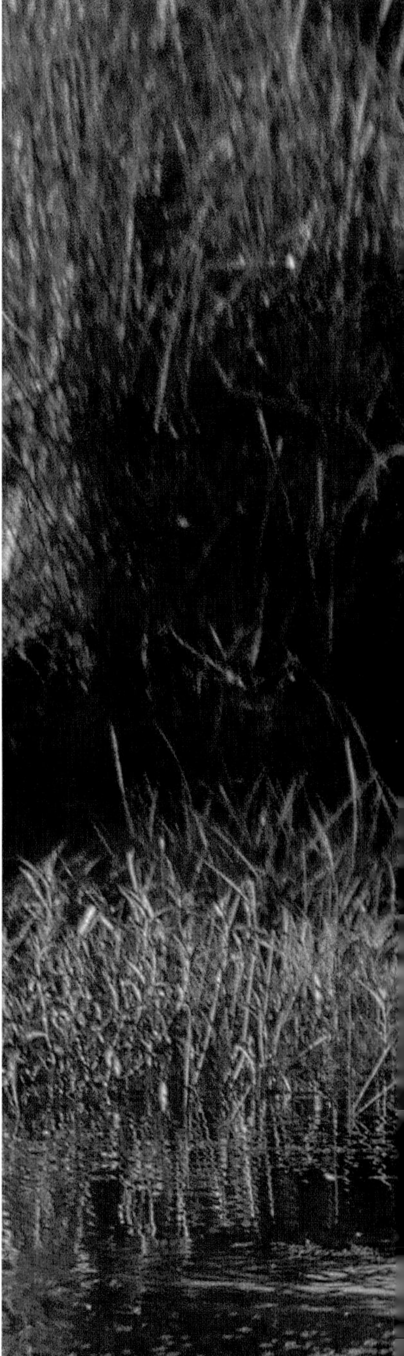

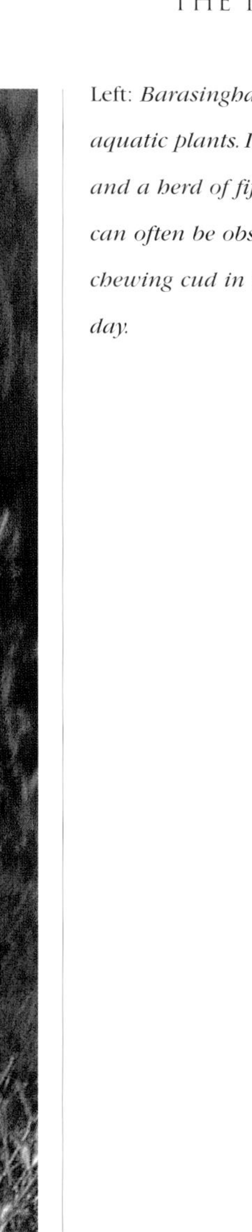

Left: *Barasingha stag feeding on aquatic plants. It is tolerant to sun and a herd of fifteen to twenty can often be observed sitting and chewing cud in the open at mid-day.*

in Hindi) pointers (*singh* in Hindi) on its splendid antlers. It is an exclusively Indian animal though some have also spilled over to the contiguous areas of southern Nepal. Its preferred habitat is an area with plenty of water and grassland. At one time, it spread across suitable habitats throughout the basins of the Indus, Ganges and Brahmaputra rivers, as well as many places in central India. Its population, however, has drastically reduced over the years and it is now found only in a very few isolated pockets. It is slightly smaller than the sambar, but in appearance it is stately and very handsome–unlike the sambar which appears somewhat unkempt.

There are two recognised races of barasingha; the swamp deer *Cervus duvaucelii duvaucelii,* dwelling in the Terai region of Uttar Pradesh, and the second subspecies *Cervus duvaucelii branderi,* found in the hard open maidans (flat grounds) of Madhya Pradesh. Once swamp deer were found in the sundarbans, but they seem to have become extinct there. The main difference which distinguishes the two subspecies is in the shape of their hooves. The swamp deer of Terai and Assam have slightly bigger and splayed hooves to support the body weight on the soft ground of the swamps, and they also have a slightly larger skull. The Madhya Pradesh race has smaller, well-knit hooves more suitable for galloping on hard ground, and it is less dependent on water.

There is a seasonal difference in the coat colour of the deer. In summer, its coat is yellowish or reddish brown on top and sides, gradually becoming lighter on the underparts. The winter coat is a heavier, coarse, dark brown in stags and a little lighter in the young stags and the does. The habitat factors also affect the colour of the coat. The Madhya Pradesh swamp deer has a darker woolly coat compared to the Terai and Assam race, which has a comparatively smoother and lighter coat. However, I have seen large stags in Kanha with very

Right: *A rutting barasingha. The tiger is the main predator of the barasingha. The deer has a very acute sense of smell, but its eyesight and hearing is moderate. Downwind, it can scent a predator from a distance and gives alarm calls with ears cocked and raised tail, while stamping the ground with a foreleg.*

dark brown coats, as well as some with light brown coats in summer. Probably the deer with dark coats were comparatively much older. The underside of the tail is white or light yellow and the tip is blackish.

The swamp deer weighs about 170 to 180 Kg (370 to 400 lb). Dunbar in his book, *Wild Animals In Central India,* quotes Dr. Blanford that two stags shot in Cooch Behar weighed 208 to 259 Kg (460 and 570 lb) respectively. These must have been exceptionally large animals. On an average the body length is about 180 cm (6 feet.), the tail length 12 to 20 cm (4.8 to 8 inches) and the height at shoulder 119 to 124 cm (3.9 to 4.1 feet). This deer is mainly a grazer and its staple food is grass and aquatic plants. It can sometimes be seen feeding in ponds and marshy wetlands with its head fully submerged in water. It is tolerant to sun and a herd of fifteen to twenty can be observed sitting and chewing cud in the open at mid-day. It generally drinks in the early morning and late afternoon. The deer has a habit of flapping its large ears back and forth in summer, which Schaller suggests is "possibly a cooling mechanism which circulates the air around the head of the animal".

The large antlers generally curve backward then almost horizontally forward, ending in line with the top of the head. After half way up the beam, tines are given off at intervals, which in turn throw off two or more pointers. The brow tines are long and are set nearly at right angles to the beam. According to Prater in *The Book Of Indian Animals,* the average antler measures 75 cm (30 inches) round the curve with a girth of 13 cm (5 inches) at mid-beam. The average number of tines is 10 to 14; Brander records that stags with 18 to 20 pointers have been shot. The antlers are at their best, hard and polished, at rutting time, and then are cast off. They start growing again within a month and the velvet is removed in due course by rubbing against grass, unlike other deer, which use the stem of a tree for the purpose.

The female comes of age at two to three years and bears one young per year. The gestation period is 240 to 250 days. The rutting time in the Terai is from September to January and in Assam, April to October. In Madhya Pradesh, where it is now found in the Kanha National Park, the rutting season is short, from mid-December to mid-January, though some stags can be heard giving rutting calls even as late as late March. Aggressive interactions between stags start at rut and soon a dominance hierarchy is established within a herd, with one stag emerging as the highest-ranking male and taking priority to any oestrous doe. It gathers a harem of a number of females, but it may not drive away those stags which have accepted their position lower down the pecking order. There is seldom a bitter fight and often the stags confront each other only in head-up display, or a short sparring match of pushing each other and twisting the head sideways. One of the challengers then disengages and coolly starts grazing with the herd, accepting its lower position. At the height of the rut, the stag jabs its antlers in grass and then struts around with pieces of grass adorning the pointers. Probably this is done to stand out and attract the females. At this time, the stag can also be found wallowing on his back in mud pools. The bugling rut call is very much like the bray of a donkey: with muzzle raised high the deer calls "ee Hohn", "ee Hohn" a number of times before gradually petering down as it gets out of breath.

The tiger is the main predator of the barasingha. The deer has a very acute sense of smell, but its eyesight and hearing is moderate. Downwind, it can scent a predator from a distance and gives alarm calls with ears cocked and raised tail, while stamping the ground with a foreleg. It also goes on full alert whenever the security system of the forest, operated by its denizens, issues warning of any predator on the prowl. It is, however, a very curious and trusting animal and sometimes overstays to check or obtain a better view. Its alarm call ranges from shrill screaming to a roaring bark.

> "it was probably one of the most spectacular wildlife sights in the world to see a herd of nearly a thousand animals galloping across a freshly burnt plain or splashing through an expanse of water in what seemed like an endless surge of antlers…"

The renowned naturalist, Billy Arjan Singh, has lamented in his book, *Tiger Haven,* that "with the possible exception of blackbuck, no other species of wildlife had been subjected to

Right: *The blackbuck is the fastest four-footed animal in the world and can sustain a speed of about 80 kph (50 mph) over a considerable distance.*

such a catastrophic reduction in numbers in the post war years". He continues "it was probably one of the most spectacular wildlife sights in the world to see a herd of nearly a thousand animals galloping across a freshly burnt plain or splashing through an expanse of water in what seemed like an endless surge of antlers..."

Those days have, regretfully, long disappeared, and the barasingha is now one of the endangered wildlife of the world today. H.S. Panwar, who was Field Director of the Kanha National Park, has recorded that in 1970 a mere 66 heads were left and that in a single congregation in Kanha National Park–their last resort. The chief reasons for the drastic decline in the population of barasingha have been the reduction and modification of their grassland habitat and heavy poaching–especially by the tribals. Sankhala, another wildlife stalwart, records that another reason has been excessive predation by tigers in Kanha, which was the result of over-baiting in the sixties in the meadows causing the tiger concentration to increase to an artificially high level. The Wildlife Department has since then intensified a number of measures, which have produced very encouraging results. A few years back it was not unusual to see herds of twenty to thirty deer grazing or resting in the Kanha meadows, but now I hardly find a few groups of four or five near the meadows. I am told that due to over-grazing in the meadows, the animals have moved to the Sonf and Mukki areas of the park.

Blackbuck, *Antelope cervicapra:* The blackbuck is an exclusively Indian antelope and was once the commonest wild animal in India. Its number was estimated to be about four million in the subcontinent. It was found in huge herds from the foothills of the Himalayas to Kanyakumari, from the semi-arid northwest to coastal Midnapore. It flourished from open

country and forests with grass meadows to semi-arid regions with only brackish water. Dunbar Brander writes that thousands of animals were shot in the nineteen twenties for their long spiral horns, considered trophies.

The open grassland, its main habitat, came under pressure for cultivation, cattle grazing and industrial uses, especially since Independence, and the blackbuck decreased in number rapidly, This beautiful animal, an integral part of Indian culture and mythology, now survives in a few pockets around the country due to the benevolence of some religious sects, such as Bishnois and Valas, or in isolated tracts reserved by the forest department as sanctuaries. The population may now be less than 25,000: about 15,000 concentrated in the 435 sq km (168 sq miles) covering 25 Bishnoi villages in the Jodhpur district of Rajasthan; 2000 in the 34 sq km (13 sq miles) of short grassland area of the Velavadar National Park in Gujarat; about 450 in the 217 hectares (536 acres) reserve forest of Rehkuri in Maharastra; nearly 350 in Dhankanya Vidi in Bolad Taluk in Gujarat and 250 in the Naha sanctuary in Haryana. It also survives in Point Calimere in Tamil Nadu, Ranebennur in Karnataka and a few other areas such as Rollapadu Sanctuary in Andhra Pradesh.

It is a medium-sized antelope with ringed, spirally twisted horns in a V-shaped pattern on the male buck only. A buck stands about 81cm (32 inches) at the shoulder, the length of the head & body is about 120 cm (4 feet) and the weight is 41 Kg (90 lb) with a tail of about 18 cm (7 inches). A good horn length is about 70 cm (27.5 inches); the largest known head–according to Dunbar Brander–carried horns of over 76 cm (30 inches), only slightly less than the height of the animal itself. In the first year, the horns are like those of the Indian gazelle, chinkara, without any twist. The spirals start forming from the second year and the horn develops

Above: *The blackbuck is a medium-sized antelope with ringed, spirally twisted horns in a V-shaped pattern on the male buck only.*

fully in about three years. The coat also changes from yellowish fawn on the upper portion of the body to velvety black, which has given it the name blackbuck. The lower parts are white and there is a sharp colour-divide between the upper and lower body. There is a fairly large irregular white patch around each eye, giving it a very distinctive appearance. The number of twists on the convoluted horn varies from three to five–and in some very large buck even six. The horns are larger among the North-Indian bucks and the size diminishes gradually as one goes south. The life span of the blackbuck is 12 to 15 years. There is a breed of albino blackbuck in Saurashtra region of Gujarat. I have seen many such animals in the Junagarh zoo. The then maharajahs of Bhavnagar, I believe, bred white bucks in the palace zoo.

The blackbuck is the fastest four-footed animal in the world and can sustain a speed of about 80 kph (50 mph) over a considerable distance. When alarmed or startled, it frequently goes into its famed leaping gallop, covering some 6 to 8 metres (20 to 25 feet) at each leap. A leaping blackbuck is a spectacular sight. It hardly seems to touch the ground and mostly appears to be airborne. In earlier times, Mogul emperors and Indian princes used to hunt the animal with a trained

Left: *A leaping blackbuck. As the cheetah is extinct in India, the leopard and wolf are now its main predators; the jackal, hyena, wild boar and eagle prey upon the fawns.*

cheetah *Acinonyx jubatus venaticus,* which is extinct in India today. The cheetah, now found only in Africa, was equally fast, but used to give up the chase after some time if not successful. Occasionally, being inquisitive, the blackbuck delayed its departure and that proved its nemesis. When suspicious, it sometimes jumps vertically up to investigate over longer distance. Once, at the blackbuck sanctuary at Rehekuri, I saw a herd crossing a high bushy divide by just jumping vertically over two metres in the air, one by one, and landing on the other side, hardly covering any distance.

The blackbuck usually drinks water twice a day, but it is a hardy species and can go without water for many hours or is comfortable even with brackish water. Its feces are hard and the urine concentrated; it is thus that the animal conserves body water. Its sense of hearing and scenting is moderate, but its eyesight is extremely sharp, as would be expected for self-preservation in an animal of grass and scrubland.

The blackbuck generally breeds in all seasons but rutting behaviour is more common between February and March, the fawns being dropped by the onset of the rainy season. The gestation period is five and a half to six months, and like the goat generally, only one young is born at a time. The mother then leaves the herd and hides the newly born fawn in grass or a bush. It rejoins the herd in a few days, as soon as the youngster starts running about. During the rut, the bucks fight to establish dominance. They stalk each other in a stilted manner, head upraised and the horns touching the back. The head-up display sometimes leads to locking of horns and bitter sparring. The defeated buck is chased away and there is always only one master buck in a group, with a harem of many does. In this condition, its pre-orbital glands exude a strong-smelling, musky secretion and–like some deer–it thrashes the grass or even the bare ground with its horns.

As the cheetah is extinct in India, the leopard and wolf are now its main predators; the jackal, hyena, wild boar and eagle prey upon the fawns. The tiger has sometimes preyed upon blackbuck in Kanha, where a small number of bucks were introduced many years ago. The habitat is not very suitable for them so hardly a few survive there now. They do continue to survive in dispersed locations, especially in the villages around Jodhpur, where Bishnois predominate. The Bishnois are followers of Saint Jambeshwar Maharaj, for whom all forms of life are sacrosanct. They are aggressively protective of all plant and animal life in and around their villages, and are even ready to lay down their lives for conservation. In the 18th century, as many as 363 Bishnoi men,

Left: *The Barking deer. It can often be seen feeding in the morning and evening along the fire lines of the forests, where fresh grass springs up after the grass is burnt.*

women and children preferred to be axed down by the minions of the maharaja in Khejarali village to protect the Khejri trees from being felled. And the protective tradition continues.

Barking Deer, *Cervulus muntjac:* The barking deer is a small thickset deer–a denizen of heavily forested hilly regions, which avoids open areas. It is widely spread in India but is not found in arid areas or terai plains. It is also a native of Sri Lanka, Myanmar, Malaysia, and the islands of Java, Sumatra and Borneo of Indonesia. It is a very shy animal of solitary habits, which is generally found singly or in pairs. A family group of three to four may also sometimes be encountered. Its coat is uniform reddish-brown in colour, somewhat darker down the spine, with white underparts and dark forelegs. A buck is about 51 to 61 cm (21 to 24 inches) at the shoulder and may weigh about 22 kg (50 lb); the female is about 7 kg (about 15.5 lb) lighter and some 7.5 cm (3 inches) less in height. It is a territorial animal very averse to leaving its home range. In addition to grass, it also feeds on flowers, leaves and a variety of wild fruits. It can often be seen feeding in the morning and evening along the fire lines of the forests, where fresh grass springs up after the grass is burnt.

The buck carries small antlers not more than 13 cm (5 inches) in length, slightly curving inwards near the tip. They are mounted on abnormally long pedicels about 8 to 10 cm (3 to 4 inches) high, which are covered with thick, rubber-like skin. Each antler carries a short brow-tine on the unbranched beam. The pedicels continue on each side of the forehead in converging ridges and hence it is also sometimes called the rib-faced deer. In fact, the barking deer is a primitive member of the Cervidae family and represents the transition phase. A thick black line runs along the inside of the facial rib and is continued along the inside of each pedicel, diffusing near the nose; the facial rib in females ends in a small tuft of bristly hair. The barking deer sheds the horns in summer; they start reforming at the beginning of the rainy season and the velvet is clear before the rains are over.

The cold weather is generally the rutting season, when the males fight fiercely for the possession of does. They sometimes inflict serious wounds on each other with their long upper tusks, which are used as a weapon of offence; the antlers are seldom used for this purpose. The tusks, or canines, are very sharp and protrude down about 1.3 cm (0.5 inches). They are not firmly rooted to the jaw, but are held securely by surrounding tissues and are movable. Dunbar Brander, who shot and studied a large number of barking deer and also kept a pet deer, writes that it possesses three cries, which –although all different–are of the same nature. Most commonly heard is the loud sharp bark, very much like that of a dog, which it gives at intervals when disturbed or alarmed. Another cry of alarm is a series of continuous short cackling barks uttered when galloping away. The rutting call, is similar to the alarm call but louder and more prolonged.

During the rut, the buck's large facial glands exude a strong smelling secretion, which attracts the females. The gestation period is about six months and one or two fawns, which are spotted, are dropped at a time, mostly in the hot weather. The barking deers chief predators are leopards, wild dogs and occasionally tiger. It is known as the watchman of the forest and its astonishingly loud alarm call reverberates over a wide area, alerting the herbivores of any danger. Sometimes, however, it keeps on repeating its alarm calls for long periods for no apparent reason at all. It can run quite fast for its size over a short distance. It has an extraordinarily long tongue, with which it can lick most of its face.

Right: *The hog deer, unlike the spotted deer, is not gregarious and prefers to lead a solitary life. The social unit is the mother with her fawn; sometimes a yearling may also accompany the female.*

Hog Deer, *Axis porcinus:* The hog deer is a primitive member of the Cervidae family, like the barking deer and musk deer, and represents the transition phase of the group. Its name comes from its squat frame and its manner of moving through the forest. It is found only in the foothills of the Himalayas, limited to some grassy plains bordering rivers. Though once it was widely found in the grasslands of north India - from Sind and Punjab to Assam and extending up to Myanmar, Thailand & Indochina - it is now confined to limited areas with riverine and swampy meadows. Such areas are also much sought after for cultivation purposes, and the wildlife has been the loser. Poaching also has adversely affected it. Though not yet endangered, its population has been steadily decreasing. The best places to observe this animal are the protected areas of Corbett & Dudhwa in Uttar Pradesh; Jaldapara in West Bengal; Manas, Kaziranga & Orang in Assam and Chitwan in Nepal.

Though a close relative of the spotted deer–and it has even been reported that they can interbreed–its general behaviour in many ways is different. Unlike the spotted deer, which runs in springing bounds leaping over obstacles, when alarmed, the hog deer crashes through the undergrowth with its head held low like a wild boar. It has relatively short legs, which are lower in the front than the back. Its height at the shoulder varies from 60 to 75 cm (2 to 2.5 feet), the body length from 105 to 115 cm (3.5 to 3.8 feet), the tail length is 20 cm (8 inches) and its weight is 36 to 50 kg (79 to 110 lb). The coat is yellowish brown and may carry barely visible white spots, particularly in the summer; the older males have darker shades. The coat has a somewhat speckled appearance, as the tips of the hair are of a very light colour, almost white. The diet of the hog deer is grass, leaves, flowers and fruits. Its sight is very sharp, and so are its powers of scenting and hearing.

“Poaching also has adversely affected it. Though not yet endangered, its population has been steadily decreasing.”

The male bears a three-tined antler on each side, set upon a long bony pedicel, which is shed in early spring. Another set of new horns grow fully again within three months. Average horns, according to Prater, measure 30 to 38 cm (12 to 15 inches). The largest Indian head has been quoted at 49.5 cm (19.5 inches) The rutting season is September and October and the gestation period is about eight months. The fawns, one or rarely two, are usually dropped in April and May and are spotted like that of spotted deer. New born fawns, however, are sometimes seen with the mother even as early as

February. The inter-birth interval is reported to vary between 243 and 316 days. Schaller has recorded that the rutting period in Uttar Pradesh seemed to run from about June to January, with a peak in September and October. The weaning period is about six months.

The hog deer, unlike the spotted deer, is not gregarious and prefers to lead a solitary life. The social unit is the mother with her fawn; sometimes a yearling may also accompany the female. It temporarily congregates into groups of 20 to 30 individuals in some open area during the rut; the assembly is primarily for selecting partners. The most dominant stag first selects a female in oestrous and leaves the area with her. This is continued till as many stags as possible acquire their mates. The hog deer does not seek a harem and has no mating call. When alarmed it raises its tail, occasionally stamps the ground with the fore foot, and makes a whistling vocalization and sharp barks. The tiger and leopard are the main predators; sometimes the python also catches one.

Musk Deer, *Moschus moschiferus:* Taxonomically, the musk deer is placed somewhere between deer family *Cervidae* and the antelope family *Bovidae* and its status is controversial. Although called a deer, it lacks antlers but possesses tusks that, like those of the chevrotain, are used in intraspecific fighting during the rutting season. The female has a single pair of mammae to suckle the young, as compared with two pairs in the true deer. To digest its food it possesses the complex four-chambered ruminant stomach, like both the deer and the antelope. Unlike other deer, it also has a gall bladder–which is a bovine feature–and lacks the facial and foot glands that are an important characteristic of all deer. A caudal gland is situated on the underside of a short tail, which itself is virtually invisible, as it is completely buried in the long

hair of the anal region. However, what makes it unique, and threatened, is the presence of a gland beneath the abdomen, a special male characteristic, anterior to the sexual organ, which secretes the strongly scented waxy substance called musk that gives the species its name.

To anyone seeing a musk deer for the first time, it presents quite a unique sight, with its long, round-tipped ears, arched back and bounding gait. In fact it reminds one of a kangaroo, or perhaps a very enlarged version of a hare. Animals of the Indian race weigh 13 to 18 kg (28.6 to 40 lb) and measure 50 to 60 cm (20 to 23.6 inches) at the shoulder, adding another 5 cm (2 inches) or so at the croupe.

It is found in wet mountain forests, from Siberia and Korea to the Himalayas. The dwarf species, found in the further reaches of the Himalayas and the border of Tibet, grow to around 40 to 45 cm (15.7 to 17.7 inches) at the withers and sport shortish faces. The head of the Himalayan musk deer is brownish grey and the contours around the long ears, eyes and jaws are greyish-white. The throat is whitish, merging into the light brown of the underside, where a white strip extends from either side of the mouth to the eyes. Its coat in Garhwal is light brown; while in Kashmir and Ladakh it is more on the greyish side. On close scrutiny, there seem to be subtle racial differences in the species. At a glance, it is difficult to tell a male from a female musk deer and this tragically leads to the death of hundreds of females at the hands of poachers. The upper canine teeth of the male are more developed and grow to a length of 7.5 to 10 cm (3 to 4 inches). The canines are used for protection and intra-specific fights during the rutting season. Its tail, almost naked and triangular, is 4 to 5 cm (1.6 to 2 inches) long and has slits on the lateral sides, which are the opening for the caudal gland responsible for tainting the feces to mark territory.

Left: *At a glance, it is difficult to tell a male from a female musk deer and this tragically leads to the death of hundreds of females at the hands of poachers. The upper canine teeth of the male are more developed and grow to a length of 7.5 to 10 cm (3 to 4 in).*

As it has been intensively hunted for centuries, the musk deer has become a very shy and unsocial animal with crepuscular habits, being active around dawn and dusk. During the day, it tends to remain concealed in thick cover or in shallow depressions scraped in the ground. The male is strongly territorial and marks shrubs and rocks, using a secretion from the caudal gland for the purpose. Severe fights take place if one male encroaches another's territory and deep wounds can be inflicted with the canine tusks. In the Himalayas, its predators are leopards, wild dog, fox and the yellow-throated marten. In Bhutan, probably tigers also predate upon the musk deer.

Its food varies according to seasonal availability - in the summer it feeds on leaves and the tender shoots of oak, rhododendron and other tree fruits, as well as herbs and grasses. During the winter as food becomes scarce, it mostly subsists on moss, ferns and arboreal lichen. It also feeds on many herbs of medicinal value such as frageria, mountain asper and cathaclimates, which help to keep it healthy.

The rutting season of the Himalayan species is from mid-November to mid-December but could extend up to the end of January. Females remain in oestrus for one month, during which they are chased by male deer who fight for their possession. The female is ready for mating at the age of about 18 months and normally the first delivery occurs when it is about two years old, after which young may be born every year. The gestation period is 180 to 195 days and most of the young are dropped in June, though there are instances of birth taking place in July, August, and even in March.

Musk has been used in the East as an important ingredient in traditional medicines from pre-historic times. It is also largely used as a dubious aphrodisiac, a cure for fever and cough, a general stimulant and an anti-spasmodic, and in the west as a fixative in expensive perfumes.

International conscience has now been roused to protect this fast-vanishing species, which is being indiscriminately hunted because musk now commands a price ranging from $45,000 to $60,000 per kg in the international market. At the beginning of the last century, Russia, China and the Indian sub-continent exported about 1400 kg of musk every year. According to Michael Green, who has studied musk deer on a WWF project, only 21g of musk was extracted from 105 musk deer by thirty poachers. Out of every six deer killed by poachers, there is only one musk-carrying male, the rest are female and young. One can imagine the number of deer killed annually to meet the export market. Understandably, the population has dwindled rapidly. Between 1995 and 1997, according to WWF, over 1.5 tonnes of musk was exported to South Korea under falsified CITES documents, which extrapolates to approximately 200,000 musk deer. Muscone was identified as the odorous component of musk and was isolated as far back as 1906, and it has now been synthetised from marocylic and aromatic compounds and so is available for use as fixative in perfumes. However, even now about 10 kg of musk is used by French industries every year.

Its timidity combined with its remote high altitude habitat, makes it very difficult to accurately estimate its population. It is included in the IUCN Red list of threatened species. However, as long as demand for musk continues, the musk deer will be widely hunted. It is now known that it is not necessary to kill the deer to extract the musk. It can be obtained by surgical means, or by the technology of scooping out the musk from the pod by the insertion of a spatula through the external opening. In China, extensive musk deer farming is established–such farms were started in 1958 in Quang Xian with two other farms in Szechuan Province. The annual

demand for musk in China alone is between 500 and 1000 kg, but their farms produce only about 50 kg of musk each year, according to WWW Traffic Organisation.

The IUCN has classified the Siberian Musk Deer as vulnerable, while the deer in China, India, and neighbouring countries are considered to be at lower risk but are coming close to being classified as a threatened species. A report by WWF-UK and Traffic (the wildlife monitoring programme of WWF and the IUCN) states that the species is undergoing "a massive decline".

Left: *The chinkara, being a desert animal, can go without water for long periods but will drink if water is available. It derives the moisture needed from the herbage it eats.*

Chinkara, *Gazella gazella:* The chinkara is the smallest gazelle in the world. It is of slender build and looks very delicate and graceful. It is basically an animal of arid regions, which prefers the semi-desert, scrubland, and undulating country of northwestern and central India. The body is light chestnut above, with white underparts and rump. A chestnut band runs along each side of the belly, separating the light colour of the upper body from the white underparts. It has tufts of hair on its knees and noticeable glands under the eyes. A light strip runs down on each side of the face from the eye to the muzzle. The forehead, and the centre of the face between the stripes, are darker than the body. The chinkara stands about 65 cm (26 inches) at the withers and weighs about 23 kg (50 lb). Both sexes carry horns; the male has heavily ringed horns about 30 cm (12 inches) long with 15 to 25 rings they curve backward and slightly inward toward the end, like a very open "S". The horns of the female are shorter and slimmer, attaining a length of 22 cm (9 inches) and are smooth.

The chinkara does not have any particular breeding season but there are two birth peaks, the major one in April and a minor one in autumn. The gestation period is about five and a half months. The male is territorial and demarcates its territory by stations, which are repeatedly used for defecating.

It is an animal of solitary habits and generally a group consists of not more than 2 to 3 individuals. On occasions, in areas like the Bishnoi villages where it feels safe, a herd of 15 to 20 animals can be seen. It has a moderate sense of hearing, sight and smell–it depends on speed for safety and is second only to the blackbuck in this. When suspicious it gives calls, which sound like sneezing, and stamps the ground with its foreleg as a warning signal. The chinkara is a very shy animal and comes out to feed in the evenings, being extreme-

Left: *The chinkara is the smallest gazelle in the world. It is of slender build and looks very delicate and graceful. It is basically an animal of arid regions, which prefers the semi-desert, scrubland, and undulating country of northwestern and central India.*

ly wary of man, who has persecuted it for ages. Unlike the blackbuck, it avoids raiding crops near villages. When suddenly frightened it does not wait to investigate, but takes off at a tremendous speed and stops only after 180 metres (200 yards) or so, to look back. Being a desert animal, it can go without water for long periods but will drink if water is available. It derives the moisture needed from the herbage it eats, and from dew. It feeds on soft grasses, various leaves, buds, crops, and fruits such as melon and pumpkin. It always gives an appearance of restlessness and is never still; it keeps on flicking its ears or twitching its black tail. The cheetah was once its main predator, but now it falls victim to leopard and the young are preyed upon by hyenas, jackals, wild dogs, foxes and even eagles.

“The chowsingha, like the blackbuck, is an exclusively Indian animal. It is the only ruminant in the world to grow four horns.”

Four-horned Antelope or Chowsingha, *Tetracerus quadricornis:* The chowsingha, like the blackbuck, is an exclusively Indian animal. It is the only ruminant in the world to grow four horns. Literally, its name means an animal with “four horns” in Hindi. Only the male carries horns, and the front pair is very small, about 3.8 cm (1.5 inches) long; quite often they are only two bony knobs just above the eyes. The posterior horns are about 10 cm (4 inches) long, are very sharp-pointed and are used for defence. The chowsingha is about the size of the chinkara, about 65 cm (26 inches) at the shoulder, and weighs about 23 kg (50 lb). The colour of its coat is a dull light brown and it has white underparts. There is a dark streak running down the front of each leg, which is broader and more visible on the forelegs.

Its range extends from the south of The Himalayas down to the Mudumalai sanctuary in Tamil Nadu. It prefers patches of grasslands in scrub and hilly country bordering dense forests. Its food chiefly comprises dry grass, the fruits of Amla *Emblica officinalis,* the berries of *Zizyphus jujuba,* the flowers of the Mahua tree *Bassia latifolia,* and a variety of buds. The chowsingha is a thirsty animal and usually drinks at midday.

According to Prater, its breeding season is during the hot weather and the gestation period is about 6 to 8 months and 2 to 3 young are dropped from October to February. The chowsingha is a shy animal and its movements are a little jerky when walking or running. It is not gregarious and is generally found alone or in pairs. It has a habit of using the same fecal station for defecating, and these stations are sometimes used as rendezvous points. It has moderate eyesight but a good sense of hearing and smell. It stands motionless when suspicious and its alarm call is a shrill whistle somewhat similar to that of a chital hind. If danger is confirmed, it gallops off, but not to a great distance like the chinkara does. Its predators normally are leopard, wild dog or sometimes the tiger.

Nilgai or Blue Bull, *Boselaphus tragocamelus:* Nilgai is the largest antelope found in Asia and is confined only to India. It is like a horse in build, but rather ungainly in appearance with high withers and drooping quarters. The male is usually 130 to 140 cm (52 to 56 inches) high at the shoulder but the female is much smaller. The average weight of a full grown male is about 240 kg (528 lb) and of a female nearly half of this. Only the male grows horns, and the average length of each horn is about 19 cm (7.5 inches) measured along the curve in front; it is straight but tilted forward towards the end.

Right: *The chowsingha, like the blackbuck, is an exclusively Indian animal. It is the only ruminant in the world to grow four horns. Literally, its name means an animal with "four horns" in Hindi.*

The tail length is 40 to 45 cm (16 to 22 inches) and tufted at the end. Both sexes have a mane on the neck and the male grows a fairly long tuft of black coarse hair on the throat. The coat colour of the bull is dark bluish-grey or bluish-black. When observed from a distance the colouration looks almost dark blue, hence the name Nilgai, which in Hindi means "blue bull". The female and the young male are of brown to orangish-brown in colour. There is a white ring above and below each fetlock and the underparts, the lips, the chin, the lower surface of tail, inside of the ear and two spots on each cheek are white. It is widely distributed from the foothills of the Himalayas to Karnataka, but is not found in Bengal, Assam or on the Malabar Coast.

The nilgai prefers sparsely wooded hills, open scrubland

Left: *Nilgai male with a crow plucking fur for its nest. When observed from a distance the colouration looks almost dark blue, hence the name Nilgai which in Hindi means "blue bull".*

and patches of heavier forests surrounding cultivation and crops. In addition to raiding agricultural crops, it also feeds on a number of jungle fruits, such as Amla *Emblica officinalis,* Ber *Zizyphus jujuba,* the flowers of Mahua *Madhuca sps,* and on a variety of leaves and grasses. It causes immense harm to standing crops, but enjoys immunity in most parts of India. There is an erroneous belief amongst many villagers that the nilgai is a relative of the cow, which is held sacred by them. It is more diurnal in its habit than the deer and feeds for much longer hours in the morning and afternoon. It can remain without water for long periods and does not drink regularly. Normally a silent animal, it sometimes makes a low volume vocalization, including a short guttural "B-A-A-E" call when alarmed. The nilgai has good eyesight, but a moderate sense of hearing and smell. It has a habit of using the same fecal station for defecating, like some other antelopes and rhinoceros. It has a life expectancy of 20 to 30 years.

Its breeding occurs throughout the year, but the peak rutting period is December to March. The dominant male gathers a harem of up to ten females. The gestation period is 8 to 9 months and generally two calves, weighing about 7 kg (15.4 lb) each, are born at a time. As it mostly lives in areas where the tiger is absent and the leopard can seldom tackle a full-grown nilgai, it has no natural enemies to fear except man. However, near some tiger territory, such as in parks like Sariska, Ranthambhore, Panna and Shivpuri, the tiger preys upon it. When chased it gallops away even on uneven grounds, with head raised towards the sky at speeds up to 48 kph (29 mph).

Nilgiri Tahr, *Hemitragus hylocrius:* Along the southern parts of the Western Ghats at an elevation from 1200 to 1800 metres (4000 to 6000 feet) lives the Nilgiri tahr, the only mountain goat which is found south of the Himalayas. It is distinguished from its close relative, the Himalayan Tahr, by its slightly larger size, shorter and crisper coat, the rounded outer surface of its horn and by possessing only a single pair of teats. An adult male Nilgiri tahr stands about 100 cm to 110 cm (39 to 42 inches) at the shoulder and weighs about 100 kg (220 lb). The female is shorter and slighter than the male. Both sexes have a short, coarse coat and a bristly mane a few centimetres long. The coat of the sub-adult, female and young buck is uniformly dusky brown to grey-brown and the underpart is paler. As the male gets older, its coat becomes dark chocolate-brown–with a striking light saddle patch on its back and for this reason it is known as "saddle back". The very dark colour contrasts sharply with the white facial stripe that drops from the forehead towards the corners of the mouth just in front of the eyes, the white carpal patches on the front and outside of the forelegs and the almost white saddle.

Both sexes have horns; the horns of the male are thicker and longer than those of the female, reaching a maximum of nearly 40 cm (15.7 inches). The average length of a female is about 26 cm (10 inches). In earlier times, the Tahr was hunted for its horns, which were regarded as trophy. The record male horn measured 44.5 cm (17.5 inches) and that of the female 35.6 cm (14 inches). The maximum girth of male horn is 25.1 cm (17 inches) but the female's is much slimmer. The pointed horns curve uniformly back until they are almost in contact at the base and have twists.

Once abundant in the rugged hills of the Western Ghats, the Nilgiri tahr is now limited to some 17 populations in the Nilgiri, Anamalai, Palini and Highwavy hills of South India. Nearly half of its present population is concentrated along the crests of the Nilgiri hills of the Tamil Nadu and Eravikulam National Park of Kerala. It is estimated that the present population remaining may be only about 2000 individuals, fragmented in many pockets. Though protected under the Wild Life (Protection) Act of 1972, the Nilgiri tahr has long been a victim of heavy poaching by shooting and snaring. It is also facing grazing competition from domestic cattle and loss of its habitat, especially for plantations of eucalyptus and tea and hydroelectric schemes and agriculture. The survival of this endangered species is largely to be credited to the untiring

Below: *Nilgiri tahr leaping over rock.*

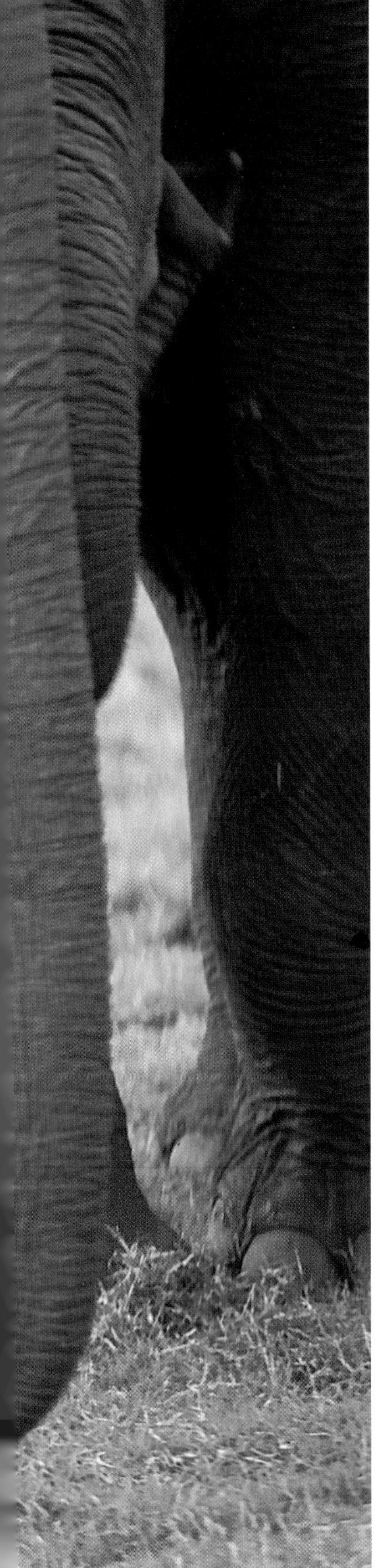

efforts of various wildlife or game associations of the South.

The Nilgiri tahr is a very shy and timid animal, very difficult to approach or spot. However, a small population at Rajamalai, near the hill resort of Munnar in Kerala, has become accustomed to man and can be closely approached. Adult males live alone or in small male groups except during the rutting period. Females and the kids live in herds of five to fifty. The tahr starts grazing at dawn and then again in late afternoon. During the hottest hours of the day, it rests in shelters in rocks and crags. It is a very alert and sharp-sighted animal. Even while resting, it keeps watch for any approaching threat and if it senses danger, it whistles an alarm and the herd immediately takes off. It is very nimble footed and quick even on very precipitous, craggy cliffs. Its natural predators are tigers, leopards and wild dogs.

It does not seem to have any definite breeding season because young are seen with the herd at most times of the year. The gestation period is said to be 180 to 242 days. The female gives birth to one or two young at a time and nurses them for about six months. Its life is between 10 to 14 years, though it is known to have survived up to 20 years in the zoo.

Elephant, *Elephas maximus:* The Indian elephant is the largest terrestrial mammal in Asia; the height of a good male is about 3 metres (10 feet) at the shoulder. The average height is 2.75 metres (9 feet), and of a female about 30 cm (1 foot) less. It is difficult to measure an elephant, but a good estimate can be arrived at by measuring the circumference of a forefoot from an impression on firm ground and doubling it. Its weight varies between 4.1 to 5.1 tonnes (4 to 5 tons). The weight of a newly born calf is about 90.7 kg (200 lb) and the height is between 76 and 91 cm (30 to 36 inches). The colour of the skin is grey to dark grey but the same animal may

Left: *Elephant society is a very stable one, where absolute discipline, loyalty and affection are the dominant characteristics. It is a matriarchal society with strong bonds between the cows, thus ensuring the well-being of the younger animals.*

appear of different colour depending upon the colour of dust or mud bath it has last taken. Once in the western zone of Kaziranga we saw a very large tusker, which was almost red! The length of the tusks, which only a male carries, is of varying size. Unlike its African sister, the Indian cow elephant has only small tusks, which hardly show. A pair of tusks kept in the Royal Museum at Bangkok in Thailand measured 3.01 m etres (9 feet 10·5 inches). The average weight of a pair is only about 45.5 kg (100 lb). The heaviest tusks in India were from a tusker shot in Terai; the length of the tusks was 8 feet 9 inches and 8 feet 6 inches, weighing 161 and 160 lb respectively. A tuskless bull, or makhna, is often a tremendously powerful animal and is feared by the other members of the herd to which it may belong. There are many instances of a makhna worsting even big tuskers in a fight.

“The elephant’s habitat has been shrinking due to human pressure and the corridors so essential for its migration have been usurped for agriculture or industrial uses.”

The multipurpose trunk of an elephant acts like its nose, giving it an exceptional sense of scenting. In addition, it is a tool for gathering food, siphoning water into the mouth and general cleaning, as well as a formidable weapon. The eyesight is rather limited to a maximum range of about 46 metres (50 yards) or so, but its sense of hearing is excellent. The trunk also plays an important role in communicating with other animals by touch, scent and sound. Because of its great size, the elephant has to spend more than two-thirds of the day in foraging. It feeds on grasses, the bark of certain trees, roots, leaves and small stems. It also favours rice, banana and sugarcane where available. The daily food requirement of an adult is about 270 to 320 kg (600 to 700 lb) of green fodder and nearly 40 gallons of water. A mature male elephant is subject to a periodic condition called 'musth'. In this condition, the temples get swollen and a dark viscous fluid, of pungent odour, is exuded from a gland between the eyes and the ears on each side of the face. The phenomenon is not fully understood but it is generally believed that the condition has some bearing on sex, and such animals temporarily acquire an incredible strength and become irrational and aggressive.

Elephant society is a very stable one, where absolute discipline, loyalty and affection are the dominant characteristics. It is a matriarchal society with strong bonds between the cows, thus ensuring the well-being of the younger animals. The elephants are exclusive in their intraspecific behaviour and though different herds may briefly come together in times of need, they interact with some reservations. Group defence, if any member is in danger, is also a basic attribute. A kinship group comprises a number of family groups, which are further divided into units and subunits. As the inter-related group grows, it breaks into smaller units in its never-ending search for food. A family unit consists of a matriarch, its daughters and grandchildren and the size can vary from three to ten or more members spread over three generations. A basic subunit consists of a cow with its unweaned calf and sometimes an older calf. The gestation period lasts for about 22 months and an adult female gives birth every 4 years starting between 13 to 15 years. Males approaching puberty are expelled, probably as a precaution against inbreeding. The elephant vocalizes in a number of ways, such as trumpeting, squealing, grunting, roaring (indulged in by juveniles 1 to 5 years of age), and barking (under 2-month-old calves), each conveying a particular mood.

The elephant, which has a wide distribution in the Himalayan foothills, is missing from the Central Indian plateau but reappears again in Karnataka, Tamil Nadu and Kerala with its range extending up to Sri Lanka. It is found in southern Bihar, south Bengal & Orissa and there is an eastern population distributed in north Bengal, Assam and other states of eastern India. Its habitat has been shrinking due to human pressure, and the corridors so essential for its migration have been usurped for agriculture or industrial uses. It is being forced into smaller and smaller range territories. There has also been extensive poaching of the tuskers for ivory, which commands a very heavy price internationally. In 1989, an international ban was imposed on the ivory trade but the clandestine trade continues and many poaching gangs are still operating. The total population of Indian elephants is believed to be about 22,000.

Though other jungle inhabitants seldom interfere with an elephant, a hungry tiger will not hesitate to attack a solitary animal. The tiger will never let go an opportunity to prey upon calves and juveniles. J.C. Daniel in his book, *The Asian Elephant,* gives a number of recorded instances of tiger predating even upon full-grown elephants. Col Kesri Singh, in his book: *The Tiger Of Rajasthan,* has given an instance of a fight between a tiger and a big tusker in Assam. "…Some three or four years ago a tiger, having killed a baby elephant, was attacked by a tusker. Instead of trying to get clean away the tiger came at the elephant from the flank or rear, and having got on to his back raked and tore at him with his claws. The fight went on for a long time, the tusker apparently trying to dislodge the tiger by running under and against trees. He seems to have succeeded in this at least once, but only for the tiger to recover and return to the attack…In the morning the area was examined and the story reconstructed from the copious signs left about the area. The aggressor had had the best of it, for the party found the remains of the elephant calf

Above: *Male gaur in Nagarhole.*

and the dead tusker's huge bulk, atrociously torn, but the tiger had disappeared."

Gaur or Indian Bison, *Bos gaurus:* The magnificent gaur represents the wild oxen, that inhabited the old world thousands of years ago. It is also called, the Indian bison, which in fact is a misnomer. The term wild oxen does not include the true bison, which survive today only in America and Europe. The male gaur is a massive black animal with a huge head, standing up to 195 cm (6 feet 4 inches) at the shoulder, the female being about 13 cm (5 inches) shorter. The length of one of the bulls shot by Dunbar Brander in the then Central Provinces (now Madhya Pradesh), measured 2.3 metres (9 feet 4 inches), from nose to root of the tail and the length of the tail was 86 cm (2 feet 10 inches). The bull has

Left: *Gaur charging. Due to its huge size and power, the gaur has few enemies to fear except man and the tiger. It now receives protection from man so the tiger is the only predator left to fear. The tiger not only attacks younger animals but also takes on large black bulls. The tiger's technique generally is to hamstring the bull by biting through its hock.*

a shiny, black, shorthaired coat, which, in reflected light, appears deep dark blue; the cows and young bulls are dark brown. The calf has a light brown coat and lacks the white "stockings" from knees to hooves so characteristic of the older gaur. Both sexes carry horns and the record horn of a bull, measured round the curve, according to Lydekker, was 116 cm (46 inches), the average spread being about 85 cm (33 inches). The bull has large conspicuous dewlap and a muscular dorsal ridge, bestowing upon it a very powerful and distinctive appearance. The cow is substantially smaller than the bull and its dorsal ridge and dewlap are not very developed.

The gaur prefers evergreen and semi-deciduous forested hills with stretches of grass meadows up to an altitude of about 1805 metres (6000 feet) or more. In India, it is found along the foothills of the eastern Himalayas, some forests in Bihar, Orissa, Madhya Pradesh and Western Ghats southwards from Maharashtra, and in Karnataka, Tamil Nadu and Kerala. The breed in Southern India attains the largest size in India. It has also spread to Nepal, Bhutan, Myanmar, Malaysia and Indio-China. It needs a good supply of water to drink, and an abundance of grass and bamboo shoots to graze and browse. Brander has noted that, in addition to various grasses and leaves, it also eats the bark of a variety of trees such as Haldu *Adina cardifolia* and fruits of Phetra *Randia dumetirum* and Bel *Aegle marmelos*. In protected areas, the gaur can be found in good numbers at the salt licks provided for wildlife. The salt works as purgative to get rid of internal parasites. It is also often found associating with wild elephants. The elephants pull down bamboo plants in their search for food, thus providing the gaur access to high bamboo leaves, which normally would have been out of its reach. The gaur feeds very early in the mornings and then is out again late in the evenings. During the hot part of the day, it retreats deep into forests to rest and ruminate. It is a very shy and timid animal, which avoids man. It is not given to crop raiding, unlike its other family member, the wild buffalo, which takes every opportunity to enter agricultural fields to feed.

The gaur is not territorial and moves about more widely than other ungulates. This is probably because of its much larger requirement for food. Schaller records that the herd size varies from 2 to 40 animals and averages 8 to 100 individuals. The rutting season in central India starts in the winter and creeps into mid-June, with a peak period in mating observed during December and January. The gestation period is about nine months and most of the calves are dropped in August and September although newborn calves are seen almost throughout the year. The cow has her first parturition at about 3 years of age and then gives birth to one calf at a time every third year. The number of bulls in a herd changes with the time of the year. During the rut, a dominant black bull remains with the herd and has first right to mate, though there could be more than one bull moving with the herd. The dominance is established by lateral display and real fight is rare. A line of hierarchy amongst the bulls is established within a herd and once accepted, the bulls lower in rank are allowed to stay. When a black bull becomes very old and past his reproductive powers, younger animals drive him out. He then leads a solitary life.

Due to its huge size and power, the gaur has few enemies to fear except man and the tiger. It now receives protection from man so the tiger is the only predator left to fear. The tiger not only attacks younger animals but also takes on large black bulls. The tiger's technique generally is to hamstring the bull by biting through its hock; the animal becomes helpless when reduced to three legs. Other threats to the gaur are habitat fragmentation due to human interference, and diseases transmitted from domestic cattle, which sometimes enter the forest for grazing. The gaur population is known to have been almost decimated, down to only a few animals, having suffered from rinderpest and foot-and-mouth diseases. In 1968, such an epidemic almost wiped out most of the population of gaur from the forests of Bandipur in Karnataka and Mudumalai in Tamil Nadu. Though a good recovery has been made since then the pre-1968 population is still far off.

Wild Buffalo, *Bubalus bubalis:* The wild buffalo, like gaur, belongs to the oxen family, whose original home was northern Asia. From there, they are believed to have spread into Europe and North America, and later into the tropical coun-

Below: *The wild buffalo is dangerous and is known to viciously charge without provocation.*

tries. Now the wild buffalo is found only in India and Nepal. The wild population found elsewhere in Asia, Australasia and Brazil are the descendants of either translocated or feral breeds. In India, the wild buffalo is mainly found in the Bastar district of Madhya Pradesh, the Manas and Kaziranga parks of Assam and the Lali Sanctuary of Arunachal Pradesh. It is a huge, slatey black animal with short, wiry and scanty hair–a large portion of its body is bare and glossy. The legs are dirty white from above the hooves up to the knees. A newly born calf is almost yellow in colour. The average height of a buffalo at the shoulder is 170 cm (5 feet 6 inches) and may reach even 200 cm (6 feet. 6 inches). The body length measures 2.5 to 3 metres (8.2 to 9.8 feet) and the tail, which ends in a bushy tuft on the tip, measures 0.5 to 1 metres (1.6 to 3 feet). The average weight of a buffalo is about 900 kg (2000 lb). It has thick black horns, triangular in section, which sweep in an outward curve back towards the shoulder. A good head may measure from tip to tip about 2.75 metres (9 feet). The horns of the female are comparatively slender but the spread can be more than the bull. It has broad splayed feet suitable for living in a marshy habitat. It has a poor power of hearing, and moderate sight, but excellent sense of scenting.

Its preferred habitat is large swamps, reed-beds and high grass, and, in the eastern region, the edges of rivers and pools. Its main food is grass but it also eats twigs, shoots and the leaves of bamboo and water vegetation. Unlike gaur, the wild buffalo does not shun man and raids cultivations in the night doing great harm to the crops. It likes to feed in the morning and again in the evening and at night. The day it spends chewing cud, sleeping, wallowing in the mud or submerged in pools to avoid being pestered by insects. It is gregarious in habit and lives in small herds of ten to fifteen cows. In the rutting season, generally in the autumn, the bulls fight

Right: *Wild Buffaloes fighting. Unlike gaur, the wild buffalo does not shun man and raids cultivations in the night doing great harm to the crops.*

to take possession of a herd. After the breeding season is over, the bulls become solitary or join large bachelor herds. Some breeding takes place at any time of the year. The gestation period is about ten months and usually there is only one calf per birth. The calf is able to stand in about thirty minutes and to suckle within an hour. Weaning occurs in about six to nine months, but it starts to graze from the time it is four weeks old. The birth interval is about 2 years.

The wild buffalo is dangerous and is known to viciously charge without provocation. In the earlier times of 'shikar', even domestic buffaloes were used to drive out a wounded tiger from its cover. On sensing the tiger, they form a line facing the animal and charge with noses out and horns laid

back. The tiger is their only predator but only a very large and experienced tiger will take them on, usually by hamstringing the hind legs first. Its population is on the decline, mainly because of habitat destruction and degradation. In addition, the pure stock of the wild buffalo is being lost due to interbreeding with domestic buffaloes. It is very susceptible to cattle diseases transmitted from village animals.

Great Indian Onehorned Rhinoceros, *Rhinoceros unicornis:* Out of the five species of rhinoceros in the world, three species were found in India. However now only the Great

Indian Rhinoceros survives, the other two, the Javan Rhinoceros *R. sondaicus* and the Asiatic Two-horned Rhino, *Didermocerus sumatrensis*, are extinct in India. The Great Indian Rhino is bigger than the Black Rhino but slightly smaller than the White Rhino of Africa. The Indian species is a massive, brownish-grey animal, standing about 180 cm (6 feet) at the shoulder. The colour varies according to the colour of the mud in which it has last wallowed. Its body length is about 350 cm (11.7 feet), the tail length 70 cm (28 inches) and weighs around 2000 kg (4400 lb). It has a grotesque appearance, almost prehistoric, with its thick skin heavily folded behind the shoulders and in front of the thighs, dividing its tubercle-studded skin into great shields. Both sexes have one horn which is not a true horn like those of a deer, antelope or ox, but consists of compressed hair cemented together in a hard compacted shape. The horn of the rhino is not firmly rooted to the skull but is epidermal and rests in the flesh. It usually avoids using it for any offensive action, preferring to employ its large incisor teeth for this purpose. The average horn measures approximately 20 cm (8 inches); the record horn of an Indian rhino kept in the British Museum is 61 cm (24 inches).

Left: *The great Indian onehorned rhinoceros has a grotesque appearance, almost prehistoric, with its thick skin heavily folded behind the shoulders and in front of the thighs, dividing its tubercle-studded skin into great shields.*

Once the rhino ranged from the northwestern passes of India along the Gangetic plain to Bihar, Bengal and Assam. The invader, Timur the Lame, is said to have hunted rhinos on the frontier of Kashmir in AD 1398. The mogul Emperor, Babur, has recorded hunting rhinos near the river Indus in 1519 in his memoirs. The rhinoceros, however, now survives in India only in a few reserves in Dudhwa, in north Bengal in Jaldapara Sanctuary, Assam in Kaziranga, and in Orang and Manas National Parks. The total population is estimated to be around 1500 in India and 400 rhino in neighbouring Nepal. It disappeared from the west mainly because of indiscriminate hunting, and loss of habitat due to clearance for cultivation, irrigation and human settlement.

The bull is generally a solitary animal though the female and sub-adults are rarely alone. It prefers tall elephant grass and reed beds in swamps, but is also found in forest ravines and low hill areas. Its diet consists of grass, twigs, aquatic plants such as water hyacinth, shrub branches, leaves and even cultivated crops. It grabs its food by curling its semi-prehensile upper lips around it and bringing it to the mouth. It sometimes submerges its entire head into the water to pull out aquatic plants. It drinks daily and is fond of visiting the salt licks. The rhino always visits definite communal fecal sites to deposit its excreta, and mounds of droppings can be observed in their habitat. It is known for several vocalizations including snorts, honks, roars and squealing. There is no particular rutting season and breeding occurs at all times of the year. Only the dominant male mates and the right is generally established by aggressive fights. The female matures around the age of six while the male does so at nearly ten years. After a gestation period of 480 days, one young is dropped per birth. At birth, the calf is about 105 cm (41 inches) in length and 60 kg (132 lb) in weight. The weaning period is 18 months and the female gives birth every three years. Usually the rhino avoids man but is known to have charged head down when harassed or wounded, or if a female with a cub is startled. A tiger will often hunt an unguarded calf.

Its life expectancy is about 40 years. The species is endangered and is included in the Red Data List of the IUCN. The hunting for sport ceased long ago but it is now under tremendous poaching pressure from highly organized gangs. There is a widely held belief in the Far East and southeast - though without any scientific basis - that the rhino horn has aphrodisiac properties. Its other body parts, including the blood, are in great demand for traditional medicines. In Yemen, the horn is highly prized for dagger handles. Early in the twentieth century, a kilo of horn was sold for UK£150 in the world market. In the 50s, the price had gone up to UK£1000. Now after processing (shaved or powdered) it has been known to reach over $45,000 per kg in the underworld markets of Taipei. Though India and Nepal are taking all precautions, poaching is still rampant. For example in 1996, poachers armed with sophisticated long range weapons killed as many as 25 rhino in the Kaziranga National Park and managed to extract horn from 21 of these.

Below: *A wild boar pair. Ferocious fights amongst the males take place to establish dominance and the right to choose the best harem.*

Indian Wild Boar, *Sus scrofa:* The Indian Wild Boar is found all over India, Nepal, Sri Lanka, Indochina and Malaysia. It even lives in the Himalayas up to an altitude of 2000 metres (6560 feet). It can adjust to an extremely wide range of environments as long as a convenient water supply is available. It is found in scrub or dense forests as well as in reed beds. A good adult boar stands about 90 cm (3 feet) tall at the shoulder and may weigh 136 kg (300 lb), or more. It has a sparse coat, black in colour mixed with grey, rusty brown and whitish hairs. It possesses sharp tushes; the upper canines form tusks, which curve out and upwards. The lower canines are like razors and are kept sharp by rubbing against the upper canines. The length of a good tusk measured round the curve is about 24 cm (9.5 inches), the record for tusks being 32.1 cm (12.6 inches).

The wild boar is omnivorous and lives on roots, tubers, crops, insects, snakes, offal, carrion and even on manure. It sometimes also makes its own kills. Its indiscriminate feeding habit has enabled it to survive in a wide array of habitats. It feeds in the morning and late in the evening and living not far from villages, it raids the cultivation in the night and is capable of doing immense harm to the crops. It has an acute power of scenting and moderate powers of hearing and sight. The boar is very fond of wallowing in muddy waterholes, an activity indulged many times during summer afternoons. Ten different vocalizations have been distinguished, commonest being the usual grunting sound, which the boar makes when alarmed or charging. Once in the Bandhavgarh National Park I heard a very agonizing squealing cry for at least 15 minutes, which reverberated throughout the forest. A tigress had attacked a wild boar and had a firm hold over the victim's throat. Even after the squealing ceased, the tigress kept up the hold for another 15 to 20 minutes to make sure that life had

Right: *Wild boar drinking at a waterhole. When roused or wounded, it will not hesitate to attack an elephant and even a tiger avoids taking on an angry boar.*

really ebbed away. The wild boar's general intelligence is very high and its courage is proverbial. When roused or wounded, it will not hesitate to attack an elephant and even a tiger avoids taking on an angry boar. Brander writes about a shoot organized for the then Duke of Connought; a boar charged one of the elephants and fastened his tusk into her leg in the region of the chest. Even a gun on top of the elephant failed to stop the attack. He also notes that it was rare for anything but a large, hungry tiger to attack a full-sized boar, and there are instances on record of the tiger having been worsted. Sankhala in his book, *Tiger,* gives an instance in the Kotah forest where a tiger and a wild boar fought almost a whole night in 1961. The tiger ripped the boar open but the boar charged back and disabled the tiger. Eventually the boar was killed, but the wounded tiger was in no mood for a meal and left the victim never to return.

Above: ***Langur with young. Its predators are tiger, leopard or wild dog. I once saw a 3 metre (about 10 feet) long python swallowing a langur in the Mukki area of Kanha National Park.***

The wild boar is a very prolific breeder and 10 to 12 piglets are born every year after a gestation period of 110 to 120 days. The population is kept under control by predators like the tiger, jackal and wild dog. The mother is very protective, but on an average only half of a litter survives to maturity. Before giving birth, she makes a regular nest by pulling out long grass and arranging it in a large circular heap. She then burrows underneath and the young are born in this shelter. The young are brown with horizontal stripes. Breeding apparently takes place at all times of the year, but Brander writes that there are two seasons in which most of the young are born, namely, shortly before the rains and again after they have ceased. Ferocious fights amongst the boars take place to establish dominance and the right to choose the best harem.

Common or Hanuman Langur, *Presbytis entellus:* The Hanuman langur is found in India, Nepal, Bhutan, Tibet, Sri Lanka, Pakistan, Bangladesh, Myanmar and China. It lives in a variety of habitats including humid forests, mangrove swamps and wooded country, from 4600 metres (16,000 feet) in the Himalayas to near sea level. The name langur is derived from the Sanskrit word, langulin, which means "one having a long tail". Five species of langur live in the Indian subcontinent; the most common is the Hanuman Langur *P. entellus,* named after the loyal servant of the God Rama, whose fight with King Ravana is chronicled in the Hindu epic, *Ramayana,* written in the fifth century B.C. He is held as the supreme role model amongst the Hindus for human devotion to God. Being a mythological character, the monkey is generally looked upon as sacred and is protected in most parts of India.

The weight of an adult male varies from 9 to 16 kg (20 to 35 lb), but in the Himalayas, it grows much larger and weighs 16 to 20 kg (35 to 44 lb). The female weighs much less. The Hanuman langur is of a slender build, about 60 cm (2 feet) long with a tail slightly longer than the body. The coat colour ranges from grey to a silvery shade, with a white head but and a jet-black face. A newly born is almost black, but it turns grey, tan or brown as it matures. It has a crest of hair on the top of the head. Unlike macaque, which temporarily stores food in a cheek pouch, the langur does so in a compartment inside its large, complex stomach. This specialized stomach permits vast consumption of leaves and is the reason for its also being called 'leaf monkey'–though it also eats other food such as fruit, berries, buds, flowers and grain with an occasional munch of a locust or larva. It usually feeds in the mornings and in the evenings. It is a wasteful feeder on treetops so ungulates like the chital, sambar and nilgai assemble below to feed on the dropped leaves or fruits, which would normally have been beyond their reach. In some populations living near temples or human habitation, "hand-outs" from people constitute a good portion of the langur's diet. It moves through the forests and on the ground on four legs and also uses a leaping gait through the forest.

As its long tail signifies, the Hanuman langur is more arboreal in habit than the macaque, but they spend 2 to 4 hours at mid-day resting and grooming each other by fur picking. Such fur picking is mostly not hunting for lice or fleas as commonly believed, but is a painstaking search for fragments of skin, skin secretions and other foreign matter. This practice also reinforces the bonds between individuals. The langur lives in social groups from 18 to 25 members, which in some rare cases comprise up to 100 individuals. Males have a dominant position within a group, but females have no fixed status. Two types of groups are formed: (1) a bisexual group comprising of both sexes but with a dominant male that has reproductive monopoly over the females of the harem and (2) an all male group composed solely of adult males. Every few years, the male group attacks the bisexual group. After a bitter fight the resident male is thrown out, and the bisexual group is taken over by a new male. The new male proceeds to kill as many of its competitor's offspring as possible so that the nursing females come into oestrus again. In turn, it also remains under pressure from other males who eye its harem. The dominant and the co-dominant guard their troop tenaciously. The life within a group is peaceful, babies are taken care of communally by all the adults, and passed around amongst them. The female is ready to breed at three and a half years of age and gives birth to a single offspring after a gestation of about 200 days.

Its predators are tiger, leopard or wild dog. I once saw a 3 metre (about 10 feet) long python swallowing a langur in the Mukki area of Kanha National Park. As is known, the primates have adequate vocal sounds to talk with each other. On spotting any moving predator a grating alarm call, "khok, khok kakookho", is given and is continued till the predator disappears. Being perched in a commanding position high up on the trees and with its excellent eyesight, it can easily keep a watch to the approach of any dreaded predator. So it is a very important member of the forest security system. Like the alarm call of a sambar, the langur's call is the most reliable sign of the presence of a predator. In addition a deep guttural call "whoop whoop" can be heard in the morning or at dusk, which reverberates through the forest. Probably this call is given to maintain group cohesion.

Rhesus Monkey, *Macaca mulatta:* The name Rhesus comes from the Greek, Rhesos, the King of Thrace, who assisted Priam at Troy. Audebert, who named the species, had chosen the name arbitrarily. In 1940, it was discovered that the monkey has the same hereditary blood antigen in its blood cells as is found in humans, and the antigen has been named RH (from rhesus) factor after it. A rhesus monkey was the first monkey to be rocketed into the stratosphere. It is a rather stocky thickset animal distributed throughout the northern parts of India from the Himalayas, Assam and as far south as the river Tapti. It is also found in Myanmar and other adjoining countries. The counterpart of the rhesus in the south is the bonnet monkey, without characteristic hairstyle but with long dragging tails. The male is about 60 cm (2 feet) long, olive brown in colour, with a very short tail, and weighs 7 to 10 kg

Left: *Rhesus Macaque grooming young. As it is held sacred in most parts of its habitat in India, the monkey has lost its fear of man and sometimes makes its home near human settlements, especially near Hindu temples.*

(15 to 23 lb). The female is much smaller and lighter. Its naked face is light pink and its hair on the crown radiate backwards without any central parting. Its hindquarter has rusty orange fur, which distinguishes it from other monkeys.

The dietary habit of the rhesus monkey depends upon where it lives and the season of the year. It thrives in a variety of habitats, from ruined forts and semi-desert scrub forests to swamps and temple roofs. It can drink brackish water, so it is able to live even in the mangroves of Sundarbans, where it exists on crabs. Its diet consists of fruits, roots, herbs, seeds and insects. As it is held sacred in most parts of its habitat in India, the monkey has lost its fear of man and sometimes makes its home near human settlements, especially near Hindu temples. It takes full advantage of the tolerance displayed towards it and proves to be bad-tempered and of great nuisance value. Sometimes it snatches food from the hands of pilgrims and even attacks children. It is less arboreal and mostly terrestrial, gleaning its food from the ground so that it is not so dependent upon tree forests as is the leaf-eating langur. In the forest, the monkey generally keeps to the outskirts and avoids penetrating deep. It is not afraid to enter water and can swim on the surface as well as under-water. It lives in social groups of up to 100 individuals, based on male dominance. In large groups, sub-groups of females may split off to form another group under the leadership of another male. Like the langur, grooming takes up a major part of its daily life. In aggressive situations, the lips are retracted in a grimace to show submission. As a threat expression, it stares with open mouth but with covered teeth.

“In 1940, it was discovered that the monkey has the same hereditary blood antigen in its blood cells as is found in humans and the antigen has been named the RH (from rhesus) factor after it.”

The rhesus monkey has a highly promiscuous mating system. The females remain in their natal group with the onset of maturity but the males leave the group in which they were born shortly before adolescence to avoid in-breeding. The breeding season varies widely; populations that live where winters are very cold mate in autumn and the young are born in the spring. In areas where seasonal changes are not so pronounced, the breeding seasons are less defined. The gestation period is about 165 days and a single young is born at a time.

The tiger, leopard and wild dog are the rhesus monkey's main predators inside a forest. It was once widely used for biological, medicinal and psychological research, where the emphasis was on perception, learning and behaviour. It was in great demand for this purpose and its population depleted rapidly. However, under pressure from animal rights groups, its export from India for this purpose was banned in 1987.

Bonnet Macaque, *Macaca radiata:* The bonnet macaque is a greyish-brown monkey replacing the rhesus monkey in South India. It is found as far north as Bombay in the west and the Godavari River in the east. It gets its name from its long hair, which radiates in all directions from a whorl on its fore-crown and forms a bonnet. It has a much longer tail than the rhesus, indicative of its more arboreal habits, but this tail is not prehensile. It also lacks the orange fur on its hindquarters. This species is a denizen of both evergreen and wet deciduous forest, up to a height of 2000 m (6560 ft), and, like rhesus, inhabits urban areas also. It is medium-sized and stockily built, with well-developed cheek pouches for temporary storage of food. Its head and body length is about 60 cm (2 feet) although it is usually nearer 50 cm (20 inches); the tail length is 38 to 54cm (15 to 21 inches). The weight of an adult male is 6 to 9 kg (13 to 19 lb) and of a female between 3 to

Above: *Bonnet macaque standing with young. Troops of as many as 10 to 100 individuals live socially in highly organized groups and sub-groups, controlled by a male dominated hierarchy.*

4 kg (7 to 8 lb). It is mainly frugivorous, but also feeds on leaves, flowers, bark, insects, grubs and spiders.

Troops of as many as 10 to 100 individuals live socially in highly organized groups and sub-groups controlled by a male dominated hierarchy. Even the females in the group have a strict dominance hierarchy. The position within the hierarchy can keep on changing, depending on many factors. For instance a dominant male broke a canine but retained its rank as long it could hide this fact. However, once the secret was out, he was forced to step down to a much lower status in the group. Those animals living in the forest are quite shy, but the troops in urban areas do not fear man. They are tolerated on religious grounds, which embolden them to snatch whatever they fancy and become a great nuisance. As with other monkeys grooming is an important activity and reinforces social bonds. Communication within the group is through postures, facial expressions, gestures and vocalization, for instance lip smacking, teeth bearing in a threatening manner or eyebrow raising. The bonnet macaque mainly walks on all fours, but also runs or walks on its hind legs, particularly if it is using its forelimbs for something else such as for feeding or carrying a baby.

Sexual maturity is reached between 3 and 5 years for females and 4 to 5 years for males. Mating occurs throughout the year, with a peak between October and November. The gestation period is about 165 days and birth occurs mainly from late March to April. A number of newly-born are also seen from January onwards, it gives birth to a single baby at a time. Weaning takes place at 3 to 6 months and the young is independent in foraging food by the time it is about a year old. The young are given to playing tricks and teasing each other. They wrestle with each other and they pretend to bite each other with no end of loud chattering and make facial grimaces at each other. The average life-span of a bonnet

Right: *When annoyed or alarmed, the porcupine very rapidly backs into an enemy with erect quills, driving the quills deep into it, which can lead to severe injury or even death.*

macaque is from 12 to 15 years. Its predators are the tiger, leopard and wild dog; the jackal preys on the young, though the mother and others guard them very protectively.

Indian Porcupine, *Hysterix indica:* The head and body of the Indian porcupine measures from 70 to 90 cm (28 to 35 inches) with the tail adding an additional 8 to 10 cm (3 to 4 inches). An adult can weigh over 18 kg (40 lb). Its hair is modified to form multiple layers of extremely sharp and easily removable spines, called quills. The quill is brown or black in colour, with a bristling mantle of long and thin quills, overlapping an undergrowth of thicker and shorter quills. The short quills that are hidden beneath the longer, thinner quills can be very dangerous to an aggressor. The white, open-ended tail quills produce a rattling sound when shaken as warning to any attacker. The Indian porcupine is found all over India and although it prefers rocky and hilly country, it is adaptable to a wide range of habitats such as tropical and temperate scrublands, grasslands and forests. It is also found in the western Himalayas up to elevations of 2400 metres (8000 feet) or more. The species is distributed in southeast and central Asia and in parts of the Middle East. It is mostly a herbivore and its main food consists of all kinds of vegetables, including fruits, grains and roots. It can be very destructive to standing crops and sometimes burrows under walls or hedges. It also gnaws on bones and dropped antlers of deer in search of the mineral calcium, which helps its spines grow.

The porcupine is nocturnal in habit and during the day shelters in caves, amongst rock, in thick shrub or tall grass, or in a burrow. Prater (1965) describes a burrow excavated in Madhya Pradesh that had a gallery 18 metres (60 feet) in length, with a long entrance tunnel, multiple exits and a large inner chamber about 120 cm (4 feet) square and 45 cm (18 in) high, lying about 150 cm (5 feet) below ground level. The porcupine is usually monogamous and the parents live together with the young in the burrow. Gestation for the species averages 240 days and the brood size varies from 2 to 4 offspring per year. The young are born with their eyes open. When annoyed or alarmed, the porcupine very rapidly backs into an enemy with erect quills, driving the quills deep into it, which can lead to severe injury or even death. The quills are easily dislodged and left in the body of the enemy, and in due course the porcupine grows them again. There are many recorded cases of tigers and leopards being killed by a defending porcupine. Occasionally the injuries force the carnivores to turn into man-eaters, since they become incapable of catching their normal fleet-footed prey species. Jim Corbett in his book, *Man-eaters of Kumaon,* records that porcupine quills do not dissolve, no matter how long they are embedded in flesh. He writes: "I have extracted, possibly, a couple of hundred porcupine quills from the man-eating tigers I have shot. Many of these quills have been over nine inches in length and as thick as pencils. The majority were embedded in hard muscles, a few were wedged firmly between bones, and all were broken off short under the skin.

Unquestionably, the tigers acquired the quills when killing porcupines for food, but the question arises–to which I regret I am unable to give any satisfactory answer–why animals with the intelligence, and agility, of tigers, should have been so careless as to drive quills deep into themselves, or be so slow in their movements as to permit porcupines–whose only method of defending themselves is by walking backwards–to do so; and further, why the quills should have broken off short, for porcupine quills are not brittle."

Common Peafowl, *Pavo cristatus:* A male peacock, with its

Right: ***Because of its wonderful and spectacular appearance, the peacock has been much sought after by people all over the world. The Phoenicians brought peacocks to Egypt more than three thousand years ago.***

gorgeous, shimmering blue and oscillated train of feathers, must be one of the most beautiful birds in the world. Because of its wonderful and spectacular appearance, it has been much sought after by people all over the world. The Phoenicians brought peacocks to Egypt more than three thousand years ago. The Romans and other medieval Europeans extensively raised them as a delicacy and for ornamental purposes. In Greek mythology, the peacock was held sacred by

Left: *The peacock has religious significance in India, being associated with the God Karthikeya, and is also India's national bird.*

the goddess Hera. Hera is said to have given the bird its glittering oceilli (eye-spots), after removing them from the multi-eyed monster, Argus, when he was killed by the God Hermes. The peacock has religious significance in India, being associated with the God Karthikeya, and it is India's national bird.

The male has a 90 to 130 cm (35 to 50 inches) body and a 150 cm (60 inches) long, blue tail train with iridescent eye-spots. The feathers on the breast and the body are bright metallic blue, and the feet are grey. Both the sexes have a fan-shaped crest on the head. The female does not have a train and her plumage is brown, white and black. The male gives a ritual dance performance during the monsoon, which is their rutting season, to attract the female. The brilliantly coloured tail feathers are spread like a fan tilted over the head, and the bird goes round, and round, periodically vibrating the feathers on the train vigorously. It drops its tail after the rutting is over, and it grows again in time for the next rutting season. Its loud and grating call, "Kayon Kayon", is not worthy of such a beautiful bird. It is very timid in the wild and slinks away into the undergrowth at any human approach. Its predators are the tiger and the leopard and sudden flight with a prolonged clattering alarm call is a sure indication of the presence of a predator. Its wing-surface to body-weight ratio is not high so the bird is incapable of long sustained flight The peahen makes a shallow nest scraped in the ground in some dense thicket and lines it with sticks, leaves and grass before laying 4 to 8 brownish-buff eggs. The incubation period is 28 days. The peacock is a polygamous bird and has a harem of 2 to 5 females. Though it nests on the ground, it prefers to roost high on the trees. It is a ground feeding bird, its diet consists of seeds, fruits, other plant material, and small animals like mice, snakes and insects.

“In 1972, the Indian Government carried out a tiger census and to its shock, found that the tiger population had declined to the very low level of only 1,827!”

THE TIGER RESERVES

At the turn of the century, the tiger population is believed to have been around 40,000. Big game hunting in the name of sport and habitat destruction, mainly for timber extraction, reduced its number drastically to about 4000 by the fifties. After India's independence the turmoil of partition followed, and wildlife in India received the lowest priority in Government plans. It was more focused on development and reclamation of land, especially in the state-controlled forests, for cultivation and the resettlement of displaced people. The calls of committed Indian conservationists, such as Kailash Sankhala, Billy Arjan Singh and B. Seshadri, went unheeded.

In 1969, the International Union for the Conservation of

Left: *Elephant herd in Corbett National Park.*

Below: *Corbett National Park from 'High Point.'*

Nature (IUCN) held its international congress in New Delhi and Sankhala drew the attention of the delegates to the appallingly low tiger population in India, which had fallen to less than 300 animals. With the support of Guy Mountfort, an international conservationist, the tiger was included in the IUCN Red Book of Endangered Species, on which all nations focus their conservation programmes. In 1970, Mountfort, at a joint meeting of IUCN and World Wildlife Fund for Nature in Switzerland, made a strong plea for international support to save the Bengal tiger. His proposal for "Operation Tiger" was accepted and a million dollars was offered to the Indian Government to assist in inaugurating a project to save the tiger. In 1970, under the initiative of the late Indira Gandhi, the then Prime Minister of India, legislation was enacted ban-

Left: *Kanha National Park - Barasingha feeding in Menhar Nullah.*

ning tiger hunting and the export of tiger skins.

In 1972, the Indian Government carried out a tiger census and, to its shock, found that the tiger population had declined to only 1,827. A "Tiger Task Force" to set up Project Tiger, was constituted in the same year, with Sankhala as a member. The broad concept of "Project Tiger" was to identify selected areas in representative ecosystems as "Tiger Reserves", where total environmental protection was to be provided to the tiger. The "Task Force" prepared "management plans", and "Project Tiger" was launched at the Corbett National Park on 1 April 1973, which became one of the first nine tiger reserves. With more resources being made available, more tiger reserves have been declared from time to time and by 2002 there were 27. Soon afterwards actions were taken to identify Nagarhole in Karnataka and Parambikulam in Kerala as tiger reserves, while Bandipur and Nagarhole, being part of one ecosystem are to be considered as one reserve instead of two. Brief information on eight prominent tiger reserves, spread over the country, is given in this chapter.

Corbett National Park and Tiger Reserve: About 300 km northeast of Delhi, at the foothills of the Himalayas, lies the Corbett National Park, a park of remarkable scenic beauty. It is here that "Project Tiger" was launched on 1 April 1973. This is the region made famous by the legendary hunter-cum-author, Jim Corbett, in his book *Man-eaters of Kumaon*. It was once very popular with British hunters, including many a distinguished viceroy and other dignitaries, for shooting tigers. So many were shot there that by the thirties the situation had become alarming. On the initiative of E.A. Smythies of the Forest Service, an area of 256.59 sq km (99.07 sq miles) was demarcated in 1936 as the first national park in India under the United Provinces National Park Act. It was originally named Hailey National Park after Sir Malcolm Hailey, the then Governor of the Province. After independence, it was first renamed the Ramganga National Park in 1954-55, then later changed to Corbett National Park in 1955-56 in memory of Jim Corbett. The park is also associated with the name of F.W. Champion of the Imperial Forest Service, the pioneer of wildlife photography in India. Most of his magnificent pictures of Indian wildlife, obtained with trip-wire and powder-flash technology, were taken in these forests.

The park area was first extended to 520.6 sq km (201 sq miles) and then to the present 1318.54 sq km (509 sq miles) with the inclusion of the adjoining Sonanadi Wildlife Sanctuary. It is in a trapezoid valley in the South Patli Doon region of the Uttaranchal Pradesh. A flat valley in the Himalayan foothills is called a 'doon.' Its elevation ranges from 365 metres (1198 feet) to 1100 metres (3608 feet) above sea level and a meandering river, Ramganga, which comes down the Himalayas, flows through most parts of the park. The river is the only perennial source of water there. The topography is varied and comprises hilly and riverine areas, grasslands, plateau and ravines. About 46 sq km (18 sq miles) of the prime wildlife habitat of the park was lost in the seventies, due to the creation of a very large, multi-purpose earth dam at Kalagarh, creating a resevoir of 83 sq km (32 sq miles). Though Kalagarh is outside the park, the reservoir submerged most of the riverine grasslands of the park favoured especially by chital and hog deer and also some of the best forests. It also blocked the natural corridor for the movement of elephants in the rainy and winter seasons to the Kalagarh forests rich in their favourite food, bamboo.

“With the abundance of prey species, the tiger density here is perhaps the highest of all tiger reserves in the country.”

However, in due course the elephants established alternative but longer migration routes. The only compensation may be that the reservoir is now attracting a large number of resident and migratory water birds, mostly in winter. Crocodiles, both long-snouted gharial, *Gavialis gangeticus,* and marsh crocodile, *Crocodylus palustris,* can also be seen basking on the banks of the reservoir.

Over 50 species of mammals, 580 species of birds and 25 reptiles are found in the park. With the abundance of prey species, the tiger density here is perhaps the highest of all tiger reserves in the country. Other wildlife in the reserve include elephant, leopard, Himalayan and sloth bears, wild dog, jungle and fishing cats, hyena, jackal, red fox, spotted deer (chital), hog deer, sambar, barking deer, goral, rufous tailed hare, wild boar, crocodile and python. The rhesus macaque and common langur are ubiquitous throughout the park. On 25 May 1986, my wife Arati and I witnessed a 5 metre (16 feet) python regurgitating a full grown chital in the sal forest south of Dhikala, the tourist center inside the park. A number of pictures of the incident have been published in my book, *The Tiger Is A Gentleman*. The rich bird life includes a wide collection of woodland, wetland and grassland birds and raptors such as Steppe and fishing eagles, the osprey, crested serpent eagle and the harrier. The park has 110 species of trees dominated by the majestic *Sal Shorea robusta, Shisham Dalbergia sissoo, Pine Pinus roxburghii,* and over 33 species of bamboo and grass. The park also has an astounding abundance of insect life.

Untill recently, the Corbett National Park was free from organized poaching, which seemed to be concentrated only in Ranthambhore and a few other parks in peninsular India. The gangs, however, now seem to be shifting their activities to the Himalayan foothills. A number of elephants have been killed for ivory and deaths of a few tigers have also been reported. There has been national concern and the authorities, with the assistance of non-government organizations, are trying their best to apprehend the criminals involved.

Kanha National Park and Tiger Reserve: Kanha National Park, covering an area of 1945 sq km (750 sq miles), lies slightly east of the central Indian highlands with Vindhya Range in the north and Satpura to the south. It largely occupies the northern slopes of the main Mekal ridge in the Satpura. The western half of the park consists of the Kisli, Kanha and Mukki areas, which are part of the Banjar valley, whereas in the east beyond Mukki, lie the Bhaisanghat and Supkhar areas, which are washed by the river Halon. The core area of 940 sq km (363 sq miles) lies in the Mandla and Balaghat districts of the Madhya Pradesh. The buffer zone of 1005 sq km (388 sq miles) sprawls largely in these two districts, with a small southeastern part in the Rajnandgaon district. The elevation of the park ranges from 450 metres (1475 feet) to 950 metres (3116 feet) and the River Surpan flows through Kanha's central grasslands.

The region has been rich in wildlife since time immemorial. As the legend goes, King Dasarath in the 5000-year-old Indian epic *Ramayana*, is said to have mistakenly killed Shravan from his perch on a hillock known as "Machadongar", when Shravan came to fetch water for his blind parents from a small lake. The lake near the Kanha meadows is called Shravan Tal; tal means a large water body. Kanha is said to have been named after the ancient Indian saint Kanva who is believed to have had his hermitage here. The area was described vividly by Captain J. Forsyth in his famous travelogue, *The Highlands of Central India* (1871). Also, this was the main field of operation of Dunbar Brander,

Right: *Map illustrating the "Project Tiger" reserves. In 2002 India had a total of 578 wildlife protected areas covering 154,572.80 sq km (59,680.8 sq miles) or 4.7% of the country's geographical area. This consisted of a total of 89 National Parks and 489 Wildlife Sancturies.*

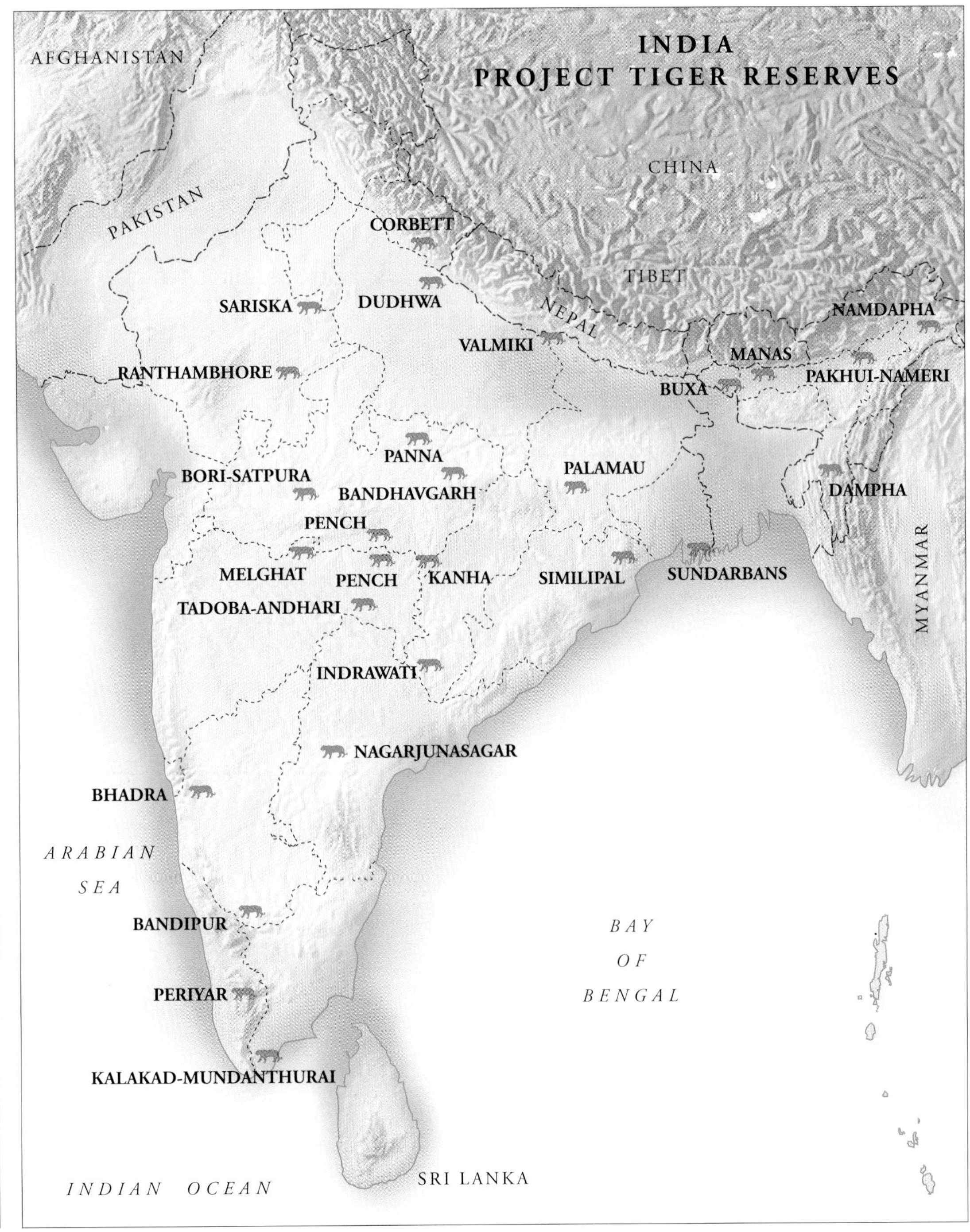

Above: *Kanha National Park - barasingha running near Mukki.*

whose book, *Wild Animals in Central India,* is considered a classic on the wildlife of the region. He wrote, "In 1900 this tract contained as much game as any tract I ever saw in the best parts of Africa in 1908. I have seen 1,500 head consisting of eleven species in an evening's stroll. It is nothing like that now, but it is probably true to say that it contains more numbers and more species than any other tract of its size in the whole of Asia." The park has a long history of conservation; as far back as 16 May 1935, two separate sanctuaries were established in the Halon and Banjar valleys having areas of 500 sq km (198 sq miles) and 253 sq km (98 sq miles) respectively. These correspond to the areas around Supkhar and Kanha in the eastern and western portions of the park. The sanctuary in the Halon valley was, however, disbanded on 26

October 1942, for alleged damage caused by the wildlife to crops and domestic livestock! The Kanha National Park was first constituted in 1955 under a special statute and the area was soon extended to 446 sq km (172 sq miles). In 1973-74, it was one of the first 9 "Project Tiger" areas selected in India. It was during 1974 that the peripheral areas selected from the Banjar valley and areas from the Halon valleys were added, to give the park its present shape.

Kanha forests are mainly composed of sal *Shorea robusta,* and mixed deciduous. The plateau is essentially grassland with sporadic growth of fruit bearing trees such as achar *Buchanania melanoxylon,* tendu *Diospyros melanoxylon* and amla *Emblica officinalis.* In the depressions below the grassland there are nullahs (water courses) with a perennial water supply. There are three large water bodies, Shravan Tal, Sondhar Tal and Kisli tank, with aquatic plants. There is Menhar nullah in the meadow, which attracts many herbivores throughout the day. This rich habitat diversity offers unique settings and ecotones supporting varied forms of plants and wildlife. There are 600 species of flowering plants, over 250 species of birds, 36 species of mammals and a good number of reptiles including the Indian python. Predators such as the tiger, leopard, wild dog, hyena, jackal, jungle cat and leopard cat, are found in the park. The prey species, sambar, chital, hard-ground barasingha, nilgai, chousingha and wild boar are also well represented. Once many blackbucks were seen in the Kanha meadows, but now these are rare.

Kanha is most famous for the tiger and the hard ground barasingha *Cervus duvauceli branderi.* Once the *branderi,* cousin of the swamp deer, dominated the central highlands, but due to the practice of baiting for tiger to attract the tourists, which led to an unusual concentration of tigers in the main habitat of the barasingha, and consequent heavy predation, only 55 survived by 1965. Habitat degradation, poaching and disease also contributed to the species reaching the brink of extinction. In the mid sixties, Schaller, the author of the classic, *The Deer and the Tiger,* drew the world's attention to the drastic decline in the population of this unique animal. In 1969, "Save the Barasingha" efforts were taken and their number has since then gone up significantly.

Bandhavgarh National Park and Tiger Reserve: North of Kanha, set amongst the Vindhya hills of Madhya Pradesh, Bandhavgarh National Park was declared a park in 1965 with an area of only 105.4 sq km (40 sq miles). But in 1982, it was extended to include two large areas of adjoining sal forests, and at present the park covers 448.84 sq km (173 sq miles). It was formerly part of the hunting preserve of the rulers of Rewa state. Rewa has always been famous for its tigers and C. Allen wrote in his book, *India of the Princes* (1984), "Nowhere were tigers more plentiful than in the large state of Rewa, where during the minority of Maharaja Gulab Singh, they had been allowed to multiply to a point where they had become a menace to the population. However, upon reaching his majority the Maharaja set about reducing their number with industry, personally disposing of 481 tigers in the first ten years of his rule." The previous ruler, Maharaja Venkat Raman Singh, had shot 111 tigers here by 1914. The ex-rulers of the state were keen to complete a bag of 109 tigers, a number considered auspicious to indicate their personal valour. The Bandhavgarh National Park is the place where the famous white tigers were discovered. The last known capture of a white tiger was in 1951. The first white tiger captured in these forests was called Mohan, and his progeny of white tigers are seen in many Indian and foreign zoos.

The historical Bandhavgarh fort, which is the nucleus of

Right: *A view of Bandhavgarh National Park showing the Chakradhara grassland with the Bandhavgarh hill in the background.*

the park, is situated on a broad plateau with an elevation of 811.4 metres (2662 feet) above mean sea level. It has steep rocks, which serve as ramparts on all sides. The fort is surrounded by 32 other hills and each of these hillocks has its own religious background going back many millenniums. The fort and the hills have a large number of caves belonging to the prehistoric period of Indian history, and some have inscriptions in ancient scripts. There are three types of forests - sal, mixed and grassland - in the park. Sal forests, broken by deciduous forests, cover about 59 per cent of the area. On the southern and western areas of the park, mixed forests with dense bamboo understorey replace sal forest. Grassland, locally known as 'bahs' occurs along the River Charanganga, which originates in the fort area and flows down the park, and along certain other nullahas. A wide spectrum of wildlife is found in the park and the jewel, of course, is the tiger. Other carnivores include leopard, hyena, jackal, wild dog, fox, jungle cat, mongoose and bear. The prey species are represented by sambar, chital, chinkara, nilgai, barking deer, chowsingha, wild boar, langur, rhesus monkey, common hare and porcupine. A checklist of 150 bird species has been compiled in the park, including the large Malabar pied hornbill and the paradise flycatcher. Reptiles, such as cobra, krait, viper, python and lizards, are also common.

The Bandhavgarh Park became internationally known because of a tigress named Sita, who could be seen almost daily in the Chakradhara and Gopalpur grasslands. She had given birth to 18 tigers over a period of 11 years. The territorial tiger was called Banka (unique one); his area was then taken over by another very large tiger called Charger. Some poaching has been suspected in the park, because the aging Banka and his two grown up cubs vanished without any trace between November 1991 and February 1992. Sita was also last

Right: *Ranthambhore National Park with Rajbagh Lake and the Fort in the background.*

spotted on June 30, the day the park closed for four months of the rainy season. She may have died of natural causes, since she was about 17 years of age, a year more than the normal life span of tigers in the wild.

Ranthambhore National Park and Tiger Reserve: The Ranthambhore forests, located in the southeast of Rajasthan, were the private shooting preserve of the rulers of the erstwhile Jaipur state. The forests lie at the junction of the Aravalli and Vindhya Range of hills, about 14 km (9 miles) from the township of Sawai Madhopur. The historic fort of Ranthambhore inside the park, from which the park derives its name, was built by the Chauhan rulers of Ajmer, in 944 AD.

The ruins of this fort now dominate the approach to the park. The fort is atop a rocky plateau about 481 metres (1578 feet) high and inside it are still seen the ruins of palaces, tombs, numerous Hindu and Jain temples and the dargah of a Muslim saint. In 1955 these forests became the Sawai Madhopur Wildlife Sanctuary with an area of 127 km (79 miles) and were designated a National Park in 1980. In 1984, the adjoining forests became the Sawai Man Singh Sanctuary and the Keladevi Sanctuary. These sanctuaries plus some other protected forests, were merged with the National Park in 1992 to constitute the present Ranthambhore Tiger Reserve, which has a total area of 1334.64 sq km (515 sq miles). The National park is managed as a core area of 274 sq km (106 sq miles), while the remaining area is managed as a buffer area to the National Park. One of the biggest achievements of the management was the relocation outside the park of 16 villages that had existed within it. The credit for this goes to the then Director of the park, Fateh Singh Rathore, who executed this policy of resettlement, involving delicate human problems, at great personal risk. By thwarting human interference with nature, he was able, within the short period of 10 years, to instill the confidence in the usually shy wildlife, including the tiger, to come out even during daytime. An old rest house, called Jogi Mahal, located at the foot of the fort, gives a magnificent view of Padam Talao, one of the three large lakes in the park. Behind the Jogi Mahal is one of the biggest banyan trees in India, with hundreds of supporting aerial roots.

The park sprawls over a highly undulating topography, varying from gentle slopes to vertical rocky escarpments, from the flat-topped hills of the Vindhyas to the conical hillocks and sharp ridges of Aravalis, from wide and flat valleys to narrow rocky ravines. The forests are of dry deciduous type and the prominent species is Dhok *Anogeissus pen-*

dula, Ronj *Acacia leucophloea,* Ber *Zizyphus maurantiana,* and Salai *Boswellia serrata.* The climate is dry sub-tropical and can be harsh, with the highest temperature reaching 47°C during summer. There are dry stretches, interspersed with streambed bearing perennial water holes. Apart from many waterholes, there are three lakes and half a dozen anicuts, which are important habitats for the wildlife. But droughts are not uncommon and during summer in some areas the animals have to move long distances in search of water.

Ranthambhore has become famous for its tigers, which have become diurnal in habit and are used to tourist vehicles. The leopard is the second largest predator in these forests. Other predators are the hyena, jackal, jungle cat and caracal. The sloth bear can also be sighted, mostly at night. The lakes and the anicuts harbour marsh crocodiles, soft-shell turtles and a variety of fish. Over the years, the crocodile population has appreciably increased and encounters have sometimes been witnessed between a tiger and a crocodile trying to take possession of a deer kill. The herbivores are led by the largest Indian deer, the sambar, which can be seen in good numbers especially around or in the lake feeding on aquatic plants. The chital is also common and nilgai, chinkara, wild boar and langur are frequently seen. Bird life is also aplenty and 264 species have been sighted here.

"The historic fort of Ranthambhore inside the park, from which the park derives its name, was built by the Chauhan rulers of Ajmer, in 944 AD."

In the first census of tigers 27 years ago, the tiger population in the park was estimated at 14. In 1991 the number went up to 45. On our visit to the park in March 1987, we saw and photographed 9 different tigers in one day! But then poachers took a heavy toll of tigers, and within a couple of years the tiger population was reduced to 15. There was a national uproar and one Gopal Mogia, belonging to the shikari caste, was arrested. He was employed by an organized gang with headquarters at Delhi. Security was increased and the tiger population is again on the increase - by 1997 the census figure was 32 tigers.

Sariska National Park and Tiger Reserve: The forests of Sariska were once the private hunting ground of the rulers of the princely state of Alwar. Apart from wildlife, Sariska has a sense of history about it going back to the Gupta period. The ruins of Hindu and Jain temples abound in the archaeological complex of Garh-Rajore, belonging to a period between the 8th and 10th century. A 17th-century castle on a sharp hilltop of Kanakwadi tells the grim story of Dara Shikoh, who was imprisoned there for years by his brother, Mughal emperor Aurangzeb. There is an ancient Hanuman temple inside the park, which attracts thousands of devotees on every Saturday. Pandupol derives its name from the pandavas of the very ancient Indian epic of Mahabharat, who, as the legend goes, lived here for sometime.

Right: *Sariska National Park with deer drinking at Kalighati.*

Sariska is at the northern end of the Aravalli range, which cuts across Rajasthan, and sprawls across 866 sq km (334 sq miles) of project area with a core area of 497 sq km (192 sq miles). The terrain truly reflects the Aravalli character, with numerous rocky valleys, cliff tops, steep escarpments, well-wooded hills and grasslands. It is covered with dry tropical forests, both dry deciduous and thorn forests dominated by dhok, and palm trees with belts of salai *Boswellia serrata* on steep dry slopes. Khair *Acacia catechu* occurs in valley beds. There are three distinct seasons: winter, summer and monsoon. Winter is severe, when the temperature can fall below 0°C. In the summer months of May-June, temperatures soar to

47°C. With an average rainfall of only 650 mm (25.5 inches) in the monsoon, there is limited natural water supply in the park. After independence, these forests were first given a Reserve status in 1955 and were upgraded to that of a Sanctuary in 1958. Sariska Tiger Reserve was created in 1978 under Project Tiger, and was declared a National park in 1982. The final notification comes into force when a few villages inside the park are relocated outside.

Sariska forests were always good tiger country, with an excellent prey base. Unlike the Ranthambhore Tiger Reserve, the tiger here, due to human disturbance, is largely nocturnal. The leopard, caracal, jungle cat, hyena, jackal and sloth bear

are among the other carnivores of the reserve. Once live baiting was carried out to attract tigers for the benefit of visitors, a practice abandoned after Sariska became a tiger reserve. Amongst the herbivores, sambar and chital are plentiful and nilgai, chowsingha, chinkara and wild boar are also common. Langurs are specially seen near the temples visited by the pilgrims and have become unusually bold. The Reserve supports over 100 species of birds. Common species are partridge (grey and black), red spurfowl, sandgrouse, flycatcher, bee-eater, great horned owl, tree pie and crested bunting. The population of peacock, grey partridges and bush quail is conspicuous.

“Once live baiting was done to attract tigers for the benefit of visitors, a practice abandoned after Sariska became a tiger reserve.”

There are many serious problems with this reserve. The water supply is very limited, although the management has tried to provide a number of artificial water holes fed by underground pipes and anicuts. These are the best places to watch the wildlife, especially during the summer. Pilgrims visiting the Pandupol temple cause much disturbance to the wildlife. A couple of state highways cross the Reserve, and the traffic has claimed many chital, and even a tiger and three leopards in the past. Sariska faces the most serious mining problems of all the tiger reserves, a survey in 1989 showed that over 200 mines fall in the protected area and over 40 in the partly protected area. Mining interests are a powerful lobby and sometimes have political support, causing problems for the management. The late Mr. S. Deb Roy, who was a Member of the Steering Committee of Project Tiger once stated, “There is probably no denying the fact that this magnificent and rugged area has recently seen serious set backs for the tiger as a result of man's greed for extracting natural resources. It is interesting to note that some local people (NGOs) have approached the Supreme Court in an attempt to stop this rampage. But it should have been the endeavour and constitutional duty of the Government to ensure safe custody of the rich national heritage here."

Manas National Park and Tiger Reserve: Manas is one of the most picturesque of India's Tiger Reserves, which sprawls over 2837 sq km (1095 sq miles) with a core area of 520 sq km (200 sq miles), at the foot of the Bhutan Himalayas. It is situated in the Kamrup-Golpara district of Assam on India's Northeast, wth the river Brahmaputra flowing on the south and the river Manas on the north of the reserve. It was previously known as North Kamrup, Manas, and became a sanctuary on 1 October 1928; parts of it had been notified earlier as reserved forests in 1907 and 1927. It was declared a Project Tiger reserve in April 1973, with Manas sanctuary as its core. In 1985 it was declared a world heritage site and, with the addition of some reserve forests, was declared as Manas National Park in 1990. The river Manas flows through the western portion of the reserve, and the reserve continues across the international border into Bhutan, where it is known as the Royal Manas National Park. The river, which has legendary association with the goddess Manasa, comes down the Eastern Himalayas bringing an enormous amount of silt and rock debris. It splits into three separate rivers and merges in Brahmaputra some 64 km (40 miles) to the south.

The reserve consists of nearly 55 per cent of moist mixed deciduous and dense evergreen forests, shisham and khair jungles, and 45 per cent of grasslands and stone and shingle -covered riverbeds. There are intermediate stages of succession-deciduous forest, swampy reedlands and sal forests in the drier areas of the reserve. Manas was one of the first nine

Left: *Manas National Park.*

tiger reserves, selected for its biodiversity of both flora and fauna. A total of 55 species of mammal, 36 reptiles and 3 amphibians have been recorded here. It has 22 species of fauna that are globally endangered. In addition to the tiger, it has its own peculiar faunal features – the rarest of which are hispid hare *Caprolagus hispidus,* the pygmy hog *Sus salvanius,* and the golden langur *Presbytis geei.* The hispid hare, also known as the "Assam rabbit", is so called because of its shaggy, bristly hair. The pygmy is a tiny wild pig no bigger than 25.4 cm (10 inches) but similar to its larger cousin. The female has only three pairs of teats compared to usual six.

The golden langur was first photographed by E.P. Gee, a tea planter of Assam, in November 1953, who brought it to the notice of the scientific community so the langur is named after him. The reserve is also noted for its wild buffaloes *Bubalus bubalis,* which are of the purest breed and attain their biggest development here with the largest sweep of horns. The great one-horned rhinoceros, the wild elephant, the gaur, the rare clouded leopard, the swamp deer and sambar and hog deer are also found in the reserve. Over 300 species of birds have been recorded, including the threatened Bengal florican *Houbaropsis bengalensis,* great pied hornbill *Buceros bicornis,* and the pied harrier *Circus melanoleucos.* Reptiles include the vine snake *Ahaetulla nasutas,* the flying snake *Chrysopelia ornate,* the Assam trinket snake *Elaphe frenata and the* gharial *Gavialis gangeticus.*

The reserve has been under tremendous pressure since February 1989, when it was occupied by local heavily-armed Bodo militants, who killed a range officer and 11 wildlife guards. This led to 30 of the 44 range posts being abandoned by forest staff. Indiscriminate slaughter of deer and wildlife took place and organised timber, rhino and elephant poachers operated freely inside the park. Intervention by either the Assam State Government or Central Government was delayed due to lack of manpower and political difficulties.

Periyar National Park and Tiger Reserve: The Periyar River in Kerala rises in the Shivagiri part of the Cardamom hills in the Western Ghats, and then meanders into the Arabian Sea. A British engineer, Col. J Pennycuick, dammed the river in 1895 and through a subterranean tunnel 1810 metres (5938 feet) long, diverted most of the water into the Vaigai River, which emptys into the Bay of Bengal. It was indeed a remarkable piece of engineering. The artificial lake, or reservoir, formed spans 26 sq km (10 sq miles). The region surrounding the lake is very picturesque and extremely rich in floral and faunal wealth. The then Maharaja of Travancore declared it a protected area in 1899 and in 1934 it was proclaimed a sanctuary. It was then called Nellikkampetty Sanctuary and covered 600 sq km (231 sq miles). It was renamed Periyar in 1950, a tiger project area in 1978 and a national park in 1982. The Periyar Tiger Reserve spreads over an area of 777 sq km (300 sq miles) with a core area of 350 sq km (135 sq miles), which is the national park. The forests are a blend of tropical evergreen, semi-evergreen and moist deciduous forests, interspersed with extensive grasslands on the upper slopes. The terrain is generally hilly and the only flat areas of the reserve are the grasslands near the edge of the lake, which lead to very dense forests providing a sustaining environment to the wildlife of the reserve. The reservoir lies at an altitude of 850 metres (2800 feet) and is the heart of the park. Its shore is broken by numerous creeks, bays and promontories. The hills in the reserve rise up to about 2016 metres (6614 feet) above sea level.

The reserve is home to nearly 49 different species of mammal. It is perhaps the best place to observe and photograph wild elephant, gaur and sambar at close range, from the safety of a boat. Often wild dog and sounders of wild pigs can also be seen. One has to be very lucky to see a tiger but on occasions in summer, one comes to the reservoir to drink. Other denizens of the park include leopard, barking deer, mouse deer, Nilgiri tahr, common and clawless otter, Nilgiri langur, lion-tailed and bonnet macaque, sloth bear and large brown and small Travancore flying squirrel. There are over 265 species of birds in the park including the Nilgiri wood pigeon, blue-winged parakeet, white-bellied tree pie, chestnut-bellied nuthatch, greyheaded myna, laughing thrush and great malabar hornbill, in addition to the usual water and woodland birds, and freshwater tortoises often bask on the deadwood of trees. There are 35 species of reptiles including the monitor lizard, python, king cobra, flying lizards with orange or yellow wings, brilliantly coloured flying snakes and the incredible flying frog. So far 1963 species of flowering plants have been documented, some of the important species are *Hopea parviflora, Dipterocarpus indicus, Palaquium ellipticum, Veteria indica* and *Myristica dacty loides.*

Once large tuskers were seen in good numbers but organized poaching for ivory has reduced their numbers considerably. The 90 km boundary of the reserve contiguous with the Tamil Nadu forests and the inhospitable terrain makes protection difficult. The electric lines inside the reserve are over-ground and a number of elephants and other animals have been electrocuted. Illegal marihuana cultivation is also being carried out in the deep interior of the park, which gives more scope for wildlife poaching. Project Tiger management, despite their constraint of staff and funds, is taking necessary action and action points have been identified.

Bandipur National Park and Tiger Reserve: Bandipur once used to be the private game preserve of the erstwhile Maharajah of Mysore. A sanctuary with 90 sq km (35 sq miles) was first created in the Bandipur reserve forest in 1931. It became the sanctum sanctorum of the earlier 800 sq km (308 sq miles) Venugopala Wildlife Park in 1973, when it was called the Bandipur Tiger Reserve. It was given the status of a National Park in 1985, though some legal formalities were pending. The Bandipur and Nagarhole forests in the state of Karnataka, Mudumalai in Tamil Nadu and Wynad forests in Kerala are a single ecological continuum, though they are being administered separately. This vast expanse is the home of a rich and varied wildlife, representing almost all the species of peninsular India.

The terrain of Bandipur is gently undulating and is broken by chains of hills, plateaus and watercourses. The highest hill in the reserve is Gopalaswamy Betta, which is 1454.5 metres (4771 feet) above sea level, and the lowest is about 780 metres (2559 feet) along the Waranchi stream. The total area of the reserve is 866 sq km (334 sq miles), with a core of 523 sq km (202 sq miles). The main rivers are the Nugu, Moyar and Kabini. The Nugu River flows through the middle of the reserve, while the Moyar River forms the southern border between Bandipur and Mudumalai Wildlife Sanctuary. It cuts into a gorge known as the Mysore Ditch, which is 260 metres (853 feet) deep and forms one of the most picturesque spots in the backdrop of the lofty bluish Nilgiri hills. Rolling Rocks is another beautiful spot on the banks of the Kakkanahalla Stream, where rocks roll down the turbulent stream during the rainy season. The Kabini River, which was dammed in 1974 at Beechanahalli for a major irrigation facility, separates Bandipur from the Naagarhole National Park.

The forest types are dry deciduous, southern tropical dry deciduous and southern tropical moist mixed deciduous. The dry deciduous teak and miscellaneous forests of the Western Ghat make it an attractive habitat for the tiger, with a rich prey base. As per the 1997 census, there were 75 tigers in the Bandipur tiger reserve. The Bandipur has more open grass and woodlands and it is easier to see wildlife here than in Nagarhole, where the forests are dense and tree canopy generally two-storied. Elephants assemble in the wet season in Bandipur, and as the summer sets in and water becomes scarce, big herds of elephants congregate in Mastigudi around the Kabini reservoir. Gaur *bos gaurus,* is another main attraction in the reserve. A severe outbreak of rinderpest had

Right: *Bandipur National Park with a view of Rolling Rocks.*

almost wiped out the population of gaur in 1968, but slowly it has made a recovery. There is a good prey base, with sambar, chital, barking deer, mouse deer, chowsingha, wild boar, langur, bonnet macaque and porcupine. In addition to the tiger, predators are represented by leopard, wild dog, hyena, jackal, sloth bear, jungle cat and ruddy mongoose. There are more than 200 species of bird life in these forests. In addition to the usual species, the Malabar trogon, blue-bearded bee-eater, Indian pitta, fairy blue bird, scimitar babbler and the green imperial pigeon are also found in the reserve.

The main highway from Mysore to Ootacamond passes through the reserve, and causes disturbance to the wildlife. The poaching of tuskers from the adjoining state of Kerala has been a vexing problem for a long time.

Tiger Reserves: Year of Creation and Area

	States	Tiger Reserves	State	Total Area (Km2)
1	1973-74	Bandipur	Karnataka	866
	1999-2000	Nagarhole (extension)		643
2	1973-74	Corbett	Uttar Pradesh	1316
3	1973-74	Kanha	Madhya Pradesh	1945
4	1973-74	Manas	Assam	2840
5	1973-74	Melghat	Maharashtra	1677
6	1973-74	Palamau	Bihar	1026
7	1973-74	Ranthambhore	Rajasthan	1334
8	1973-74	Simlipal	Orissa	2750
9	1973-74	Sunderbans	West Bengal	2585
10	1978-79	Periyar	Kerela	777
11	1978-79	Sariska	Rajasthan	866
12	1982-83	Buxa	West Bengal	759
13	1982-83	Indravati	Madhya Pradesh	2799
14	1982-83	Nagarjunasagar	Andhra Pradesh	3568
15	1982-83	Namdapha	Arunachal Pradesh	1985
16	1987-88	Dudhwa	Uttar Pradesh	811
	1999-2000	Katerniaghat (Extension)		551
17	1988-89	Kalakad-Mundanthurai	Tamil Nadu	800
18	1989-90	Valmiki	Bihar	840
19	1992-93	Pench	Madhya Pradesh	758
20	1993-94	Tadoba-Andheri	Maharashtra	620
21	1993-94	Bandhavgarh	Madhya Pradesh	1162
22	1994-96	Panna	Madhya Pradesh	542
23	1994-95	Dampa	Mizoram	500
24	1998-99	Bhadra	Karnataka	492
25	1998-99	Pench	Maharashtra	257
26	1999-2000	Pakhui-Nameri	Arunachal Pradesh- Assam	1206
27	1999-2000	Bori-Satpura	Madhya Pradesh	1486
			Total	37761

Population of Tigers in Project Tiger Reserves

	Name of Reserve	1972	1979	1984	1989	1993	1995	1997
1	Bandipur (Karnataka)	10	39	53	50	66	74	75
2	Corbett (Uttar Pradesh)	44	84	90	91	123	128	138
3	Kanha (Madhya Pradesh)	43	71	109	97	100	97	114
4	Manas (Assam)	31	69	123	92	81	94	125
5	Melghat (Maharashtra)	27	63	80	77	72	71	73
6	Palamau (Bihar)	22	37	62	55	44	47	44
7	Ranthambhore (Rajasthan)	14	25	38	44	36	38	32
8	Simlipal (Orissa)	17	65	71	93	95	97	98
9	Sunderbans (West Bengal)	60	205	264	269	251	242	263
10	Periyar (Kerala)	-	34	44	45	30	39	40
11	Sariska (Rajasthan)	-	19	26	19	24	25	24
12	Buxa (West Bengal)	-	-	15	33	29	31	32
13	Indravati (Madhya Pradesh)	-	-	38	28	18	15	15
14	Nagarjuna sagar (Andhra Pradesh)	-	-	65	94	44	34	39
15	Namdhapa (Arunachal Pradesh)	-	-	43	47	47	52	57
16	Dudhwa (Uttar Pradesh)	-	-	-	90	94	98	104
17	Kalakad (Tamil Nadu)	-	-	-	22	17	16	28
18	Valmiki (Bihar)	-	-	-	81	49	N.R.	53
19	Pench (Madhya Pradesh)	-	-	-	-	39	27	29
20	Tadoba (Maharashtra)	-	-	-	-	34	36	42
21	Bandhavgarh (Madhya Pradesh)	-	-	-	-	41	46	46
22	Panna (Madhya Pradesh)	-	-	-	-	25	22	22
23	Dampha (Mizoram)	-	-	-	-	7	4	5
	Total	**268**	**711**	**1121**	**1327**	**1366**	**1333**	**1498**

N.R. – Not reported by the State.

Population of Tigers in India

	Name of State	1972	1979	1984	1989	1993	1997
1	Tamil Nadu	33	65	97	95	97	62
2	Maharashtra	160	174	301	417	276	257
3	West Bengal	73	296	352	353	335	361
4	Karnataka	102	156	202	257	305	350
5	Bihar	85	110	138	157	137	103
6	Assam	147	300	376	376	325	458
7	Rajasthan	74	79	96	99	64	58
8	Madhya Pradesh	457	529	786	985	912	927
9	Uttar Pradesh	262	487	698	735	465	475
10	Andhra Pradesh	35	148	164	235	197	171
11	Mizoram	-	65	33	18	28	12
12	Gujarat	8	7	9	9	5	1
13	Goa Daman & Diu	-	-	-	2	3	6
14	Orissa	142	173	202	243	226	194
15	Kerala	60	134	89	45	57	73
	Total	**1638**	**2732**	**3543**	**4026**	**3432**	**3508**
16	Meghalaya	32	35	125	34	53	*
17	Manipur	1	10	6	31	-	*
18	Tripura	7	6	5	-	-	*
19	Nagaland	80	102	104	104	83	*
20	Arunachal Pradesh	69	139	219	135	180	*
21	Sikkim	-	-	2	4	2	*
22	Haryana	-	-	1	-	-	N.R.
	Total	**189**	**92**	**462**	**308**	**318**	

N.R. - Not reported by State

* Tiger census was not carried out in North East States in 1997

TABLE SOURCE: PROJECT TIGER STATUS REPORTS

Left: *A very large and angry tiger approached, coming within two metres (6 feet) of us.*

"My success ratio over the whole project was about one tiger in six days - and that doesn't mean all the photographs were usable!"

PHOTOGRAPHING TIGERS

According to the 1997 census, the population of tiger in India was 3508; out of that 1498 were to be found in the then 23 main Project Tiger Reserves. Unless favoured by an unusual piece of luck, one may be in for a bad disappointment if one just goes to a tiger reserve with the hope of photographing a tiger. Tigers are extremely shy, secretive and private animals, with nocturnal habits in most of the forests in which they live. The biggest problem for the aspiring photographer, therefore, is to locate a tiger, and then to approach it. We have been regularly visiting Bandipur Tiger Reserve, in Karnataka, for the last thirty years but have not seen even a single tiger there. The reserve had 75 tigers in 1997. We go there to photograph wild elephants, gaur and wild dogs

Left: *A fine study as a tiger yawns. Preoccupied in his own world he gives no evidence of being disturbed by the photographer.*

Some Tiger Areas: Tigers can be seen in the Corbett Tiger Reserve, if one spends a week or so there. It may, however, be just a fleeting glimpse - not enough to obtain a good picture. On our visits to the Corbett since 1974, we have seen a number of tigers in the grasslands, the forests or drinking at the Ramganga River from a distance. It was only once, on 27 April, 1988, that we were able to take some satisfying pictures of a tiger near the Khinanouli area. The tiger was sitting near a nullah for about two hours ignoring our presence. Brijendra Singh, the Hon. Wildlife Warden of the park, who was with us, even filmed the tiger.

In my experience, the best places to photograph wild tigers are Bandhavgarh, Kanha, and Ranthambhore Tiger Reserves, in that order. Bandhavgarh is spread over 1162 sq km (449 sq miles), but tigers are easily seen in a small area at the foothills of the Bandhavgarh fort in the grasslands of Chakradhara, in Gopalpur or the nearby forests in Bhadrashila and Dhobiakhol. The tigers in these areas are the progeny of a tigress christened Sita by the forest staff, and her mates known as Banka and Charger. Banka took over the territory after the death of a tiger called Daddy in 1984, and Sita and Banka had many litters. Over the years Banka and Sita had grown very tolerant to the departmental elephants and jeeps carrying tourists. Another very large tiger appeared on the scene in December 1990, and it took this tiger more than a year to drive away the dominant tiger, Banka, and take over his territory. Being a new tiger from another area of the park, he was not familiar with the elephants or the vehicles and savagely charged them, hence he was given the name Charger. My wife Arati and I had a very frightening experience on 6 March, 1992, when Charger attacked me while I was trying to photograph him. I have written about this in my book, *The Tiger Is A Gentleman*. In fact this was our one and only bad experience with a tiger, though we have seen about 150 different tigers in the wild and photographed about 100 of them! In due course Charger settled down and raised four litters with Sita. Sita was last seen in June 1998 then disappeared; she was already 16 years of age - rather too old for the wild. On 16 February, 2000, Charger had a fight with two other tigers and was badly injured. On and off, the Wildlife Department tried to take care of him, but he breathed his last on 29 September, 2000. But the grown up cubs of Charger from Mohini, daughter of Sita, have now established their territories here. All the tigers, that grew up as cubs in Chakradhara and adjoining areas have been accustomed to seeing tame elephants and vehicles since their early cubhood. They take no special notice of tourists and photographers and permit close approach. Before dawn, a number of elephants with very experienced mahouts are sent into the reserve to locate a tiger. Once located, the "tiger show" starts and tourists are taken to and fro to see the tiger on the departmental elephants. In the afternoons one can take a drive in the jeep. I have dwelt in some depth on the reasons why Bandhavgarh, in my opinion, is the best area for tiger photography. A word of caution though - after all, these are all wild tigers and sometimes may not be seen for days on end! 'Nick' Nichols, the staff photographer of the *National Geographic*, spent nearly two years on a project to photograph tigers. He has this to say: "My success ratio over the whole project was about one tiger in six days – and that doesn't mean all the photographs were usable!" Incidentally, he shot 1800 rolls of film on this assignment.

> **"In my experience, the best places to photograph wild tigers are Bandhavgarh, Kanha, and Ranthambhore Tiger Reserves, in that order"**

The Kanha Tiger Reserve, even at the turn of the last century, was long famous for its tigers. It was long preserved as the exclusive shooting area of the most privileged. Now the reserve harbours 114 tigers, as per the 1997 tiger census. Here also the "tiger show" is organized by the management and tourists are taken to see the tiger on elephants. It is difficult to take interesting and action pictures of tigers during these organized shows, but one can see them and take pictures. I generally wait till the last tourist has departed. I then take an elephant ride and wait for the tiger to become somewhat more active. The authorities sometimes give permission for this, if they are convinced that one is a serious naturalist and

Below: *Photographing a tiger with our mahout Kuttappan on Dodua Hills.*

Above: *The camera's reward. A beautiful study of a tiger in repose during the heat of the day.*

wildlife photographer. We have done our best tiger photography by taking an elephant ride in the afternoons and taking a chance on locating a tiger with the help of the "jungle alarm system" operated by the herbivores and the birds. Visits to two areas called Badi Chuhri and Choti Chuhri, or the Kanha meadows have sometimes been very fruitful when we have looked into the shady spots of the various nullahs. In the summer heat, tigers sometimes lie in small pools of water, cooling themselves. Sometimes, with prior permission, we take a ride on one of the elephants which leave before dawn to locate tigers for the tiger show. If the tiger is located, good action photography is possible in the early morning light before the tourists arrive. At the entrance to the reserve is Kisli, which is a hilly area with dense forests. Elephants may be available more easily in Kisli, as the main rush of tourists is in the Kanha area. I have done some satisfying tiger photography in Kisli.

If there is a tourist pressure, and the show continues for a long period, the elephants get tired and are allowed to rest in the afternoon. One can then take long drives inside the reserve and many times we have also taken good tiger pictures from a jeep. Photography from a moving vehicle is hardly ever satisfactory; it is advisable to stop the vehicle and switch off the engine.

A few years ago the Ranthambhore Tiger Reserve was a paradise for wildlife photographers keen to photograph tigers. We first visited the reserve on 16 March, 1987, and stayed in the picturesque Jogi Mahal, overlooking the Padam Talao (the lotus lake). At that time, Fateh Singh Rathore was the Director of the park. We could photograph nine tigers in a single day during our short stay there. They completely ignored us and went about their daily chores confidently. But within a couple of years, organized poaching took a heavy toll of tigers and their population decreased drastically. Strict precautions were taken and the tiger population is now steadily increasing. On a visit in January 2000, we saw many tigers and photographed a tigress and her three 9-month-old cubs. Ranthambhore is again a good reserve for tiger photography, where tigers can be seen in their normal pursuits such as stalking, hunting or taking care of their young. However, due to heavy vehicle pressure inside the park and limited routes being available, the management allots a particular route to a vehicle and free movement is not allowed.

> “The tigers are generally found in the grassland where the prey base graze. This sanctuary, therefore, has the highest density of tigers per unit area.”

Generally late March or early April is a good period for

tiger photography. Due to water scarcity and heat, there is a better opportunity to find tigers around the few waterholes or the pools in the nullahs. The undergrowth is also dried, giving better visibility. The background, however, may be dry and not green. Once it rains, there are pools of water even in the hilly areas and the tiger need not come down to drink, especially when it is with a kill.

Orang Wildlife Sanctuary in Assam is a very small protected area of only 75 sq km (29 sq miles), out of which 45 sq km (17 sq miles) is grassland and the remaining 30 sq km (12 sq miles) woodland on higher levels. It was declared a reserved forest in 1915, and a wildlife sanctuary on 20 September, 1985 with a tiger population of 17. In 1988, the number had increased to more than 20 tigers. The tigers are generally found in the grassland, where the prey base graze. This sanctuary, therefore, has the highest density of tigers per unit area. We visited Orang, which is 85 km (53 miles) from Tezpur, in January 1986 and again in February 1988, and found it a very good place for photographing tiger, one-horned rhinoceros and hog deer. But being a very small place, it does not have tourist facilities and special permission to visit is required. Like the Manas National Park, Orang has also been a politically disturbed area for the last few years.

Jungle Lore: Once a "Tiger Show" is on, the tiger has already been located, otherwise one is on one's own. Looking for a tiger in a vast forest area is like looking for a needle in a haystack. It is very useful to be able to identify the various calls one hears inside a jungle, especially the alarm calls of the denizens indicating presence of a predator. A security system operates in the jungle, which is operated by the prey species both at ground level and at height. The ungulates keep a watch from the ground and the langur and monkey from the treetops. A metallic call "ponk" or "dhank" by a sambar, especially if repeated again after a short interval, is a sure indication of a tiger on the prowl. A high-pitched "Ku, Ku, Ku" call of chital could mean the presence of a predator, but not always. I have heard it issue alarm on missing its fawn. Once, on hearing repeated calls, we hurried inside a sal forest just to find a rutting chital stag with its mate! If more than one chital call, a tiger or a leopard is nearby. The alarm call of a barking deer is like that of a dog, but the call may only be an alert and does not necessarily mean sighting of a predator. Peafowl suddenly flying away calling, or langurs giving excited calls of "Kho ka kookho" from treetops, indicate the movement of a predator. While driving in the reserve, the behavior of the wildlife may also be carefully watched. If the deer are standing motionless with their tail up, rump showing, stamping the ground with their forelegs and looking in a certain direction, it means a danger has been sensed and the photographer should wait and watch for a possible opportunity. Chances of success can be improved by anticipating the path of a predator on the move.

Equipment: The range of cameras and accessories is vast these days, and every year a new model with many new features appears in the market. My first camera was a Nikon F3 with manual focus lenses. In due course I have gone through many new models and now use Nikon F5 and Nikon F90X cameras, and many new automatic and some old, larger manual lenses. It does not mean that there are no other good makes: my first camera was a Nikon and I had Nikon lenses.

Left: *Charger attacking me on 6 March, 1992. Arati and I were in the grasslands of Chakradhara on an elephant called, Siddhanath, with the well-known head mahout of Bandhavgarh, Kuttappan. The incident was described in detail in my book* The Tiger Is A Gentleman. *I felt the full blast of the foul smell from the tiger's breath, and spots of frothy saliva fell over my clothes. Kuttappan shouted loudly and threw a stick at Charger, which distracted him from pressing his attack. Charger caught the stick and chewed it to pieces. He then abruptly turned and went back into the grass cover and roared deafeningly.*

It was, therefore, logical that I continued with the Nikon system, as replacing the system would have been rather costly and I was satisfied with the results. The lenses play a more important role than the camera itself, and the faster a lens the better for wildlife photography. Autofocus lenses are preferable to manual lenses for action photography, as time is not lost in focusing manually.

I prefer the F90X camera for tiger photography, as its weight is quite manageable on an elephant with one hand holding the camera. The elephant is never still and the tiger is usually under cover with low available light. As my main interest is action photography, I use only 35 mm cameras. They are highly portable and better suited for action photography. I normally set the camera to matrix metering.

I generally use 100 ASA Fuji films, but keep some 200 ASA films for emergency. Again, it is not because other 35 mm films are not as good, but I have used Fuji films for a long time so even before clicking the shutter, just by looking into the viewfinder, I know how the picture is going to turn out. I always use aperture priority mode and adjust the aperture as required by the lighting situation. When taking pictures from an elephant, which is hardly ever still, it is no use coming down to 1/60 sec or lower shutter speeds as one would get a blurred image. At least 1/125 sec. shutter speed should be aimed for and, if possible, the aperture adjusted accordingly.

If on a vehicle, a proper sturdy tripod can be employed. If the picture is well composed and the lighting is acceptable, a better and sharper result can be expected with a camera support. We keep a tripod and a monopod in the vehicle, but I usually always use something called a beanbag, which is a versatile camera support. The commercially-available bag consists of a strong cloth bag filled with dried beans, polystyrene beads or similar material. My wife, Arati, makes a bag at home, about 33 cm x 28 cm (13 x 11 inches) in dimension and provided with a zip. The zip is locked against accidental opening by a safety pin anchoring it. We fill the bag with rice, bean or wheat, whatever is easily available near the forest. We carry it with us even on the elephant, though it is not always practical to use it. But working from a vehicle with a bean-bag, one can get away even with $^1/_8$ sec shutter speed using a telephoto lens. The beanbag provides me with a better maneuverability for action photography. I do not find cable release practical in quick changing situations. However rifle grips are useful devices and come with an adjustable "stock" with a shoulder butt and a handgrip at the other end. I, however, use hand held cameras when on an elephant. I have

Below: *Tourists being taken for Tiger Show.*

developed my own technique of using the support of a raised knee, or the shoulder of Arati or of the mahout of our elephant. If possible, I always choose a smaller elephant to ride, as I get a lower angle view of my subject.

Lenses: I find an 80-200 mm/f 2.8 zoom lens most useful for photography from elephant-top. If the lighting is very good, even a 75-300 mm lens, or a 300 mm/f4 give very satisfactory results without shake. It is advisable to keep a short zoom lens, say a 35-70 mm, readily available. In April 2001, we found two 9-month-old tiger cubs on a palas tree, while their mother had gone hunting. We could approach the tigers so closely that my 80-200mm zoom could not be used and I needed a wide-angle lens to take pictures. There are no space problems when using vehicles and even a 400 mm lens or more can be used with proper support. I leave all the heavy lenses in the vehicle, and on the elephant carry only a 80-200mm/f2.8 lens, a 300mm/f4, a 105 mm/f2.8 macro lens and a short zoom 35-70mm lens. Once I took pictures of a tigress showing affection to her cubs with a 105 mm macro lens from very close quarters, and could get greater depth of field. It is advisable to focus on the eyes, or still better on the whiskers of a tiger. A tiger image with very sharp whiskers makes a pleasing picture. But the whiskers shake as the tiger breathes and it needs a fast shutter speed to freeze the shake – rather difficult in the limited light of a jungle.

Stray Tips:

- An elephant is never still and its movement is bumpy. A few hours' ride can end with a sore body. It is advisable to relax the body and flow along with the movement.
- A detailed study of wildlife, especially on its general habit and behaviour, is extremely useful. It should, however, be

remembered that the same animal in a different habitat or circumstance may behave differently. Once we approached a tusker on our jeep in the Bandipur Tiger Reserve. The animal became irritated and gave us a fright by chasing our vehicle for quite a distance. The same tusker ignored us and allowed us to approach very closely at the Kabini reservoir end of the same reserve. It pays to talk with the mahouts and experienced vehicle drivers about what to expect in their area.

• Jungles can be very dusty and adequate precautions should be taken to protect the cameras, lenses and films against dust or unexpected rain. Before setting out in the forest every morning, or still better at the end of every trip, it is advisable to clean the camera and the lenses with a blower and a brush and also to check the camera settings.

• To capture action, I keep on looking through the viewfinder at the tiger and click when it does something interesting. As you can imagine lots of patience and time are required for action shots. If the action is very fast and very interesting, I use the motor drive.

• A tigress with cubs below one year generally hides her cubs when she goes hunting. It may take her a day or two to make a kill. On return to the general area, she gently emits a number of low pitch calls, "aaaooonh, aaaooonh", and soon the cubs come out of the bushes. The reunion scenes display affection, the animals licking each other and the cubs rubbing their body against the mother, make interesting pictures. By smelling the mother's mouth, the hungry cubs know they will get their meal. Their joy knows no bound and the record is worth several rolls of film.

• Before venturing on serious wildlife photography, one should have mastered the basic techniques of photography and the use of the camera system should be second nature. An opportunity in the jungle may never be repeated!

Right: *An elephant is never still and its movement is bumpy. A few hours ride can end with a sore body. It is advisable to relax the body to flow with the movement, and not to be stiff.*

Final Thoughts: I would like to conclude this chapter by quoting F.W. Champion, the father of wildlife photography, from his book, *With A Camera In Tigerland* (1927): "I would close this book with an appeal to others who do not enjoy spilling the blood of beautiful animals, many of which are rapidly being exterminated, to abandon the rifle in favour of the camera, the use of which provides all the pleasures and excitements so dear to the heart of the big-game hunter. Indeed, it provides others as well, for, in addition to giving one a far greater insight into Nature and all her marvellous ways, a camera in skilful hands produces pictures of great scientific value, which may give pleasure to many others in a way that mere horns and skins can never do, be they ever so large."

TIGER SUB-SPECIES AND DISTRIBUTION

THE TIGER'S TERRITORY once stretched from Eastern Turkey to Siberia, Korea, China, Indochina, and Indonesia up to India. Once a species gets so widely dispersed and isolated in remote niches, different communities of the same species evolve slight differences over a long period of time, while adjusting to the regions, biological resources and local environmental conditions. When populations of the same species are consistently different from each other, taxonomically they are called subspecies.

Carolus Linnaeus, the Swedish botanist who established the modern binomial system for classifying species, initially gave the name *Felis tigris* to the species in 1758, which was later changed to *Panthera tigris (P.t.)*. Over a period *Panthera tigris* developed into 8 subspecies.

The Siberian or Amur tiger, *P.t. altaica,* is found throughout the coniferous, scrub, oak, forests and grasslands of the Central Asian regions of Russia, Northeastern China and North Korea. This is the largest of all the other subspecies and there are records of a few specimens reaching a length of up to 4 metres (13 feet) with a maximum weight exceeding 364 kg (800 lb). In the 19th century, during the construction of the Chinese Eastern Railway, the Siberian tiger was deliberately eradicated. In recent years, after the break up of the Soviet Union, it has come under considerable poaching pressure and the number has come down considerably. In 1991, one third of the Siberian tiger population was said to have been killed to meet the demand for their bones and organs in China, Taiwan and Korea. It was estimated that in 1987, only about 200 tigers were left in the wild. With the tighter conservation measures taken since then, the population could now be nearer 300.

The orange coating of the Amur tiger is paler than that of other subspecies. The stripes are brown rather than black and are widely spaced. It is massive in appearance, carrying thick white ruff of fur around its neck.

The South China (Amoy) tiger, *P.t. amoyensis,* is distributed throughout the forests and grasslands of Central and Eastern China. In the early 1950s, the number of Amoy tiger, including the South Chinese population, was estimated to be about 4000. Since then, however, there has been a drastic reduction due to poaching, and the tiger having been declared a pest and its killing encouraged. At present its number is estimated to be at best between 30 to 50 individuals - far below that required for genetic survival so the chances of its survival are remote. In size it is smaller than the Bengal tiger, with male tiger measuring about 2.5metres (8 feet) and an average 150 kg (350 lb) in weight; and the female tiger about 2.3 metres (7.5 feet) in length and 110 kg (240 lb) in weight. The stripes are short and broad and are spaced far apart compared to other subspecies. The topcoat is reddish-ochre, and the whitish belly colours do not extend to the flanks.

The Caspian tiger, *P.t. virgata,* has become extinct in the past 50 years. It was once found in the forests and grasslands of Afghanistan, Eastern Turkey and the Central Asian regions of Russia. The colouration resembled that of the Bengal tiger, but the stripes were narrower and more brownish. The tiger had a well-developed belly mane and a short nape mane.

The Indochinese tiger, *P.t. corbetti,* is distributed in the forests, grasslands and mountain areas of Cambodia, Laos, Thailand, Vietnam, eastern Myanmar and peninsular Malaysia. The population of the *corbetti* subspecies is estimated to be close to 1000. It is slimmer and smaller than the Chinese tiger.

The Sumatran tiger, *P.t. sumatrae,* is found on the Indonesian Island of Sumatra. Its population in estimated to be about 400 to 500, all located within the five national parks in the island. It is the smallest of all the subspecies and has the darkest coat with striped forelegs. Its broad, black stripes are comparatively narrower than other tiger species.

The Javan Tigers, *P.t. sondica* lived in the Indonesian Island of Java but has now become extinct. This was in spite of the tiger being given full legal protection in an especially reserved national park. The last Javan tiger was seen in 1972.

The Balinese tiger, *P.t. balica,* once roamed in the Indonesian Island of Bali. The last Bali tiger was killed in 1937 and the subspecies is now extinct.

The Javan and Balinese tigers, like the Sumatran subspecies, have all descended from the Indochinese tiger and are smaller than other subspecies. The Balinese tiger was the smallest with the male ranging from 90 to 100 kg (200 to 250 lb) in weight and female 65 to 80 kg (140 to 175 lb). The extinction of tigers in Java and Bali is attributed to fragmentation of their habitat, drastic reduction in their prey base and hunting accelerated by civil unrest in the late 1960s.

State of the Tiger

Other than the Bengal tiger, there are seven more subspecies. Of these, three are already extinct and even zoological specimens of them are not available. The remaining five sub-species are in grave jeopardy. The South Chinese tiger may already be extinct or may survive for a couple of years more.

Siberian Tiger: There are now more Siberian tigers in zoos (about 490 in number) than in the wild. The estimate of Siberian tiger in the wild varies from 150-430 in number, fragmented over a vast area. There are three protected areas for tigers in Russia - the Sikhote-Alm (3500 sq km/1355 sq miles), Lazovsky (1170 sq km/455 sq miles), and Kedrovaya Pad (180 sq km/70 sq miles). Chinese newspapers have reported sighting of tigers in Changbaishan, near the Chinese border with Korea. The Cat Specialist Group suggests that there are fewer than fifty Siberian tigers in China, and the number is too small for long-term survival. The Siberian tiger has had legal protection since 1992, but enforcement is faltering. Poaching for tiger bones and other parts required for traditional Chinese medicines, and factors like the worsening economic situation, lessening prey species, loss of habitat, and the opening of borders to China and Korea, have meant disaster for the Siberian tiger.

The situation is unlikely to improve unless the current socio-economic situation stabilises to an extent that the federal programme for tiger conservation can be fully implemented. Relaxation of border controls and easy access to the wildlife markets of the South and Southeast has dramatically increased the poaching of Siberian tigers. "Right now we are facing a situation when the main threat to the tiger population survival is in lack of unified approach to the strategy of its conservation...The issue of sustainable forest and game management is a very crucial one," says Evgeny Stomatyui of the Russian Department of Natural Resources.

South China Tiger: At one time four of the surviving sub-species of tiger lived in China: the Siberian tiger in the far northeast bordering Russia and North Korea, the South China tiger in Central China, the Indochinese tiger in far south bordering Vietnam, Laos and Myanmar and the Bengal tiger in South Tibet and north eastern Yunnan Province.

In 1950 the population of the South China tiger was said to be more than 4000, but it was then declared as a pest and mercilessly killed. It is reported that 3000 tiger skins were collected up to 1980 and the bones were sent to pharmaceutical factories for processing into traditional medicines. The present population may be around 30 to 35 tigers in the wild. There is no precise census data available. These are said to be scattered over Hunan, Guangdong, Fujian and Jiangxi Provinces. There has been no sighting of the South China tiger for many years now, though a few tigers are reported to survive in the Jingan Mountains on Hunan's eastern border with Jiangxi Province, and the Nanling Mountains on the southern border with Guangdong Province. Though China became a signatory to CITES in 1985, it has continued the use of tiger parts for traditional medicines. China is still a major manufacturer of such medicines, which are being exported to many countries - including the USA and Canada, where a sizable ethnic population lives. The South China tiger will most probably be extinct within the next few years. It is almost certain that it will not survive to greet the year named after it.

Indochinese Tiger: The Indochinese tiger population is spread over five countries and the number may be less than 1500. Experts fear that the subspecies is disappearing faster than the other three subspecies, and every week one is trapped, shot or poisoned. Poaching is high, since most of the countries harbouring the subspecies are consumer countries and tiger products are available in local markets. There has not been any comprehensive tiger population survey in Laos (PDR), Malaysia and Myanmar, though the official figure for tiger population in Malaysia is said to be about 500 animals. Incidentally, up until 1950, the tiger in Malaysia was accorded a status lower than that given to a wild pig or bandicoot and was to be killed by every possible means. In Myanmar it is still not illegal to kill a tiger. According to the Cat Specialist Group of The World Conservation Union (IUCN), there were about 1050 to 1750 Indochinese tigers in the world, distributed in Southern Vietnam, China, and Cambodia. Laos, Thailand, Malaysia and eastern Myanmar. The main tiger areas, however, are Thailand and Malaysia. The correct status of these subspecies is unknown due to the very broad distribution in hilly forested and mountainous areas bordering many countries. Access to these areas was restricted due to wars and civil unrest, but recently scientists have been granted limited permission to carry out field survey.

Thailand: Thailand is widely considered to be the primary range of the Indochinese tiger. In 1998, the tiger population in the country was estimated to be between 250 and 500, but it is feared that the number may now be as few as 150. Though Thailand has banned the hunting of wild tiger and trade in tiger parts, the Environment Investigation Agency - a non-profit environmental organization - has documented Thailand's repeated failure to tackle the widespread illegal trade in bones and organs. In fact it has a thriving trade in both import and export of tiger products and derivatives. A number of tiger breeding centres continue to exist to clandestinely feed the factories producing tiger bone products for the domestic and international market. There is extreme, worldwide concern about the purpose and the nefarious activities of these particular breeding centres, which could provide a legal cover for the smuggling of tiger parts from other tiger countries.

Malaysia: The population of the Indochinese tiger in Malaysia is officially reported to be between 491 and 510 animals, distributed over eight different states. In 1951, Locke estimated a tiger population of 2990 in Malaysia, with the highest concentration of 1100 tigers in the State of Pahang. The forest cover then was 60 per cent, but after independence in 1957 large areas of lowland dipterocarp forests - the prime habitat of the tiger - were converted into additional rubber and oil palm plantations. Some of the tiger habitat was cleared for paddy and fruit orchards. The tiger was more and more confined to smaller forests, surrounded by farmers and their livestock. The tiger's prey-base of mainly wild pigs had almost disappeared. This precipitated increasing attacks on livestock, and in Malaysia there are no compensation schemes for farmers who lose livestock to predation.

It was a classic man-tiger conflict situation, where the tiger was ultimately always the loser. Between 1947 and 1985, as many as 378 tigers fell victim to spring guns, pit traps, poison and snares. The increasing demand for tiger body parts for Chinese traditional medicines took its heavy toll, and by 1976, the tiger population was reduced to about 300 tigers. The Department of Wildlife and National Parks of Malaysia has reported an increase in number since then. The tiger has been declared as one of the most endangered species and has been categorized as a "Totally Protected" species in Malaysia.

Mynamar: The Irrawadi River flows from north to south through the middle of Myanmar and separates the Bengal tiger, *P.t. tigris,* and the Indochinese subspecies *(P.t. corbetti).* In 1985, the tiger population in Myanmar was estimated to be about 3000, half of them Indochinese. In 1998, according to a report by Uga and Than, between 106 and 234 Indochinese tigers were living in Eastern Myanmar. The Myanmar Government has devised a comprehensive Tiger Conservation Action Plan and has placed the tiger in the "Completely Protected Category" of their Protected Species list. However, poaching and trafficking in tiger parts is rampant due to the almost open border with China.

Vietnam, Laos (PDR) and Cambodia: The Indochinese tiger is said to be found in 24 of the 87 Nature Reserves and National Parks of Vietnam, but a scientific survey to establish tiger number is only now underway. According to the Cat Specialist Group of IUCN, 200 to 300 tigers were living in seven of the Nature Reserves in 1994. Poaching for tiger parts is heavy, and the Ministry of Forestry admits that the tiger population was declining in Vietnam.

The status of the wild tiger in Laos (PDR), and Cambodia is not known. Only recently a protected area system has been introduced in Laos (PDR), while the Wildlife Department in Cambodia is non-functional. It was reported that in Cambodia, tiger products were openly sold in Phnom Penh Poipet in early 1994. In Laos (PDR), tiger was reported to be present in 17 sites, but definite signs were found only in four sites. Cambodia became a member of CITES in 1997, but due to political instability has not been able to pursue any serious conservation action. Cambodian authorities estimated in 1995 that two to three tigers were being poached every month. However, according to the Cambodia Tiger Action Plan, this figure could be at least 10 to 15 tigers per month. There have been some sightings of tigers in Laos (PDR) and the country has requested international assistance to increase its law enforcement capacity. There was a virtual absence of prey-base in all the sites. The future of the tiger appears bleak in both countries in light of the ongoing poaching.

Sumatran Tiger: Once there were three subspecies of tiger in Indonesia and numbers ran into more than two thousand. However, already two subspecies, the Javan Tiger, *P.t. sondica,* and the Balinese Tiger, *P.t. balica,* have become extinct in the last sixty-five years. The Javan Tiger was under the full protection of the Indonesian authorities as a part of their national policy at the time of its disappearance. The number of the last Indonesian subspecies, the Sumatran tiger, is down to 300 to 400 in the wild, from about 1500 individuals in 1975. It is living in five national parks and two game reserves. The largest population of about 110 tigers is found in the Gunung Leuser National Park, and the rest are distributed in smaller numbers in other parks and reserves.

The subspecies is very vulnerable and is facing similar threats to survival as tigers in other tiger countries; habitat shrinkage; prey base decrease and increased poaching. The Sumatran tiger has been classified as critically endangered by the IUCN. The Indonesian Government formulated an "Indonesian Sumatran Tiger Conservation Strategy" in 1994, highlighting the need for securing and protecting the remaining tiger population and its habitat.

BIBLIOGRAPHY

A Century of Natural History (1983). Edited by J.C.Daniel, BNHS.

Ahmad, Shahbaz (2001). *Charger*. India.

Ali, Salim (1938). *The Wild animals of India and the problems of their conservation,* J of BNHS 38 (2) :231-40.

Baker, S. (1890). *Wild beasts and their ways,* UK.

Blanford, W. (1888-91). *The fauna of British India: Mammalia,* UK.

Boswell, K. (1957). *Scent trails and poking in tiger,* J of BNHS 54(2): 452-54.

Burton, R.G. (1933). *The Book of The Tiger*. UK.

Burton, R.W. (1929). *The tiger's method of making a kill.* J.of BNHS, 33 (4)

(1948). *Wildlife Preservation in India*. J.of BNHS, 47.

Champion, F. W. (1927). *With A Camera In Tigerland,* UK.

(1934) *The Jungle In Sunlight And Shadow,* UK.

Chaturvedi, M.D. (1955). *Future of the tiger,* Indian Forester, 81, India.

(1969). *Panther On The Prowl,* India.

Corbett, J. (1944). *The Man-Eaters of Kumaon*. UK.

The Man-Eating Leopard of Rudraprayag, UK.

My India, UK.

Daniel, J.C. (1996). *The Leopard In India,* BNHS, India.

Dunbar, Brander, A.A. (1923). *Wild Animals In Central India,* UK

Encyclopedia of Indian Natural History (1986), BNHS.

Forsyth, J., Captain (1871). *The Highlands Of Central India,* UK.

Gee, E.P. (1964). *The Wildlife Of India,* UK.

Ghorpade, M.Y. (1983). *Sunlight & Shadows,* London.

Gordon, Graham B.N. (1950). *Hunter at Heart,* London.

Harrison, H. *Can Wildlife Survive In India?* International Wildlife. 5 (5):41-9.

Hewett, J. (1938). *Jungle Trails in northern India,* UK.

Hornaday, William T. (1989). *Wild Animals–Their Minds and Manners,* India.

Jerdon, T. (1874). *The mammals of India,* UK.

Krishnan, M. (1975). *India's Wildlife in 1959-70,* India.

Locke, A., Lieut. Col. (1954). *The Tigers of Trengganu,* London.

Lydekker. R. (1907). *The Game Animals of India, Burma and Tibet,* UK.

Mackay, R. D. (1967). *Have You Shot An Indian Tiger,* India.

Mountfort, Guy (1981. *Saving The Tiger,* UK.

Penny, Malcolm and Brett, Caroline (1995). *Predators,* UK.

Perry, R. (1964). *The World of the Tiger,* UK.

Perumal, T.N.A. (1990). *Photographing Wildlife in India,* India.

Pocock, R. (1929). *Tigers,* J. of BNHS 33:505-41.

Powell, A.N.W., Col. (1957). *Call Of The Tiger,* UK.

Prater, H. (1965). *The Book Of Indian Animals,* India.

Project Tiger–Status Report (2001), Govt. Of India.

Rice, W. (1857). *Tiger-shooting in India,* UK.

Rodgers, W.A., Panwar H.S., and Mathur V.B. (2002). *Wildlife Protected Area Network in India–A Review.* Wildlife Institute of India.

Saharia, V.B. (1982). *Wildlife In India,* India.

Sanderson, G (1912). *Thirteen years among the Wild beasts of India.*

Sankhala, Kailash (1978). *Tiger,* UK.

Schaller, George B. *The Deer And The Tiger,* USA.

Seshadri, B. (1986). *Call Of The Wild,* India.

Singh, Arjan (1973). *Tiger Haven,* London.

Singh, Kesri, Col. (1959). *The Tiger of Rajasthan,* UK.

Smythies, E. (1942). *Big Game Shooting in Nepal*. London.

Smythies, O. (1953). *Tiger Lady,* UK

Sterndale, R. (1884). *Natural History of Indian mammals* UK

Stewart, A. (1928). *Tiger and other game,* UK.

Stracey, P. (1961). *The future of the tiger,* The Cheetal, 3(2):29-32.

Thapar, Valmik (1986). *Tiger: Portrait of a Predator,* UK.

(1992) *The Tiger's Destiny,* UK

(1999) *Tigers: the Secret Life,* UK

Tinker, J. (1974). *Will India Save the Tiger,* New Scientist 61:802-5.

Turner, J. (1959). *Man-eaters and memories,* UK.

Ward, R (1922). *Records of Big Game*. London.

Wardrop, A.E. (1923). *Indian Big Game,* UK.,

INDEX

Acknowledgements

In the years that I have spent in wildlife photography, I have had the good fortune of meeting eminent and dedicated persons in the field. They have been a source of encouragement as well as valuable information. Among them is Mr. J. C. Daniel. He is one of the most respected naturalists of India, who was the Curator/Director of the prestigious Bombay Natural History Society for over thirty years. He has received many national and international awards for his untiring efforts in the field of conservation of endangered species. He has authored many natural history books and written over fifty research papers. I wish to thank him for writing the foreword to this book.

I also acknowledge with thanks the assistance of Mr. T. N. A. Perumal, one of the top wildlife photographers of India, for assisting me in the selection of wildlife images out of a very large collection. I would also like to thank the authors of the books mentioned in bibliography for valuable information on natural history. Significant data on wildlife was also gleaned from a very large number of wildlife sites on the intenet. I hope I would be excused for not naming individual authors or the internet sites whose help I have indirectly taken in writing this book.

I thank my son-in-law Gopal K. Saxena for assistance in finalizing the book though very hard pressed for time, being on a short business trip to India. I would also like to thank my daughter Mukta Shivanand for going through the book and making many suggestions. It would not have been possible to write this book without the meticulous on-the-spot notes of my wife Arati chronicling each jungle visit with dates during the last three decades or so. These records run into about eighty diaries and with their help I have been able to recall and relive almost every jungle experience and wildlife picture.

And finally, my grateful thanks to the unsung heroes of wildlife conservation - the forest officials - from Chief Wildlife Wardens to forest guards and mahouts. Without their support, co-operation, and wholehearted assistance, neither this book nor any worthwhile photography would have been possible.